Living the Good Life

FOREST FARM
JAMAICA, VERMONT

HELEN AND SCOTT NEARING

Living the Good Life

HOW TO LIVE SANELY AND SIMPLY

IN A TROUBLED WORLD

Introduction by PAUL GOODMAN

Schocken Books • New York

CONTENTS

a section of photographs follows page 62

"It is my purpose to lay out unto you the waies so to dwell upon, order, and maintaine a Farme, as that it may keepe and maintaine with the profit and encrease thereof, a painefull and skilfull Husbandman, and all his Familie."

Gervase Markham, The Countrey Farme, 1616

"Useful Arts are sometimes lost for want of being put into Writing. Tradition is a very slippery Tenure, and a slender Pin to bear any great Weight for a long Time . . . Whoever has made any observation or Discoveries, altho' it be but a Hint, and looks like a small Matter, yet if pursued and improved, may be of publick Service . . . I am sure I should have been glad of such an History of Facts (as imperfect as it is). It would have afforded me Light, Courage and Instruction."

Jared Eliot, Essays upon Field-Husbandry in New-England, 1760

"There can be no doubt but that many of the articles which follow in this work will appear to men who have devoted their lives to the arts and those sciences which are most immediately connected with them, as trite and little worthy of notice. But what might seem to such persons as merely commonplace information may, perhaps, prove valuable to others, whose time may have been devoted to pursuits of a different nature."

Thomas Green Fessenden, The Register of Arts, 1808

"For want of records, much useful knowledge is continually lost. Though many individuals have derived advantages to themselves from experiments, but few have recorded them. Even those who make experiments are liable to forget them, so as to give incorrect representations of them when they attempt to relate them."

Leonard E. Lathrop, The Farmer's Library, 1826

"The principal object of this work is to save young housekeepers the pain and trouble of buying their own experience; and though it is particularly addressed to those residing in the country, I have had the satisfaction of finding that it has been in many cases almost equally useful to those living in towns."

Jane Loudon, The Lady's Country Companion, 1852

"This is not to be the history of the working of a great farm run by some rich man regardless of expense, with model buildings, model machinery, and the rest. On the contrary, here is but a modest place, modestly, if sufficiently, furnished with the necessary buildings, capital, instruments, and labour. Possibly for this very reason the details connected with it may prove of the more value to readers interested in the subject."

Rider Haggard, A Farmer's Year, 1899

INTRODUCTION

I FIRST heard Scott Nearing forty years ago, when he came to lecture us students at City College. His line was a kind of deviant Marxism—he had just been expelled from the Communist Party—but he won my strong attention by the way he handled the question period. He gave reasons, he answered objections with more specific reasons, he did not resort to slogans. The result was that I took his position seriously, though I didn't become a "Marxist." I hope that, in my own talks on campuses, I sometimes have a similar thoughtful effect on one of those watchful faces who wait there saying nothing. And now I am glad to recommend to the reader the new edition of this book by Scott and his wife, Helen. It has become more important than when they wrote it.

It is chock-full of reasons—for leaving the city, for going to Vermont, and why to build with conglomerate and eat this and that. It is sometimes comically reasonable, when the "reasons" so seriously advanced might seem to the reader, as they do to me, to be the result of whim or prejudice. The Nearings find it hard to say that they do some things just because they like them that way and damn well please. Yet there is no doubt that just this stubbornness and conviction that they are in the right, are invaluable to persist for twenty years on an arduous and eccentric course and achieve something fine for themselves and relevant for everybody. Also, as I look at Scott, solid and hearty, pushing ninety—I don't know how old Helen is—I must conclude that their extreme vegetarian diet without stimulants or spices hasn't done them any harm.

The economics of *Living the Good Life* is not Marxist, not even deviant, but goes right back to Aristotle's *Oeconomica*, household and estate management, the techniques and allocation of resources and effort to get the most use and satisfaction, quite apart from market, money, profits, or reinvestment.

For a full-dress study in this kind of economics, the reader should look at Ralph Borsodi's *Prosperity and Security* that came from the same crisis of the Depression that sent the Nearings to Vermont. In my own *People or Personnel*, written a full generation later, I try to show that the same principles of small-scale operation without cash-accounting and managed by the producers themselves can be applied to many other enterprises besides family farming; such enterprises are often more efficient and productive of real goods, and give far more security and life-satisfaction, than the centralized, overplanned, and regimenting mercantilism that is now the pervasive economic style.

By 1970 it is clear that we have to take seriously the Thirties' ideas of the Nearings, Borsodi, Frank Lloyd Wright, and the Southern Regionalists—and the economic ideas of Gandhi before them and, of course, the kibbutzim. Their experiments and analyses used to seem cranky, if not crackpot, and they were certainly not in the mainstream of the technical and political issues that were discussed. But suddenly we have reached a tipping point. Ecologically, we are facing disaster, both environmentally because of pollution and physiologically because of poisoning. Abuses of technology have gone so far so fast, that the chief present purpose of technology must be to try to remedy the effects of past technology. Everywhere in the world the galloping urbanization is proving to be ecologically and fiscally unviable; worse, it is impossible to bring up citizens in urban and suburban areas that are no longer cities. The processing and social engineering that go with these conditions have called forth waves of populist protest, articulate and inarticulate, by those who are pushed around and find themselves without power. And finally, the expanding Gross National Product, the ever higher Standard of Living, which was the justification for all this, has begun to yield sharply diminishing returns, trivial goods, incompetent services, base culture, and spiralling inflation.

Thus, the eccentric ideas of the Nearings and the others are no longer out in left field. History, alas, has caught up with them. With a few more years of power failures, transit strikes, epidemics of heroin overdose, water shortage, unacceptable levels of air pollution, crashing aeroplanes, hundreds of thousands of New Yorkers will regard Scott and Helen as uncanny prophets. My own opinion is that American society would be far more viable if we could push the present five percent rural ratio back to something like twenty percent, as an option and a standard of people who respect the environment and who, as Jefferson pointed out, cannot be pushed around because they can feed their faces.

Today very many young people across the country have decided to try subsistence farming and natural foods for nearly the same reasons as the Nearings told themselves forty years ago. I don't know what influence the older writers have had. Most of the young, I am sure, imagine that they thought it up out of their own heads, just as they imagine they invented pacifism, sit-ins, self-reliance, participatory democracy, progressive education, and sexual freedom. And this is just as well; right ideas do not need authoritative antecedents. What the young can get from this book is know-how. They are, understandably, inept farmers; the Nearings are, famously, superb farmers. Certainly our communal hippies will be appalled by the Puritan rectitude of the Nearings, their extraordinary prudence in gathering stones for a ten-year building plan, their almost cash-accounting of labor time, and their rigorously hygienic pleasures. It might rub off on the young, however, that thought and responsibility are useful things even in subsistence farming. (Especially if, unlike the Nearings, they keep animals, which they are bound to do because of their loyalty to warm and furry life of all species. My friend Bob O'Brien, who breeds sheep at Tunbridge, Vermont, has complained to me that his hippie neighbors forget to feed their horse and it is pathetic.)

In one important respect, there is a striking difference in life-theory between the Nearings and the furry generation of emigrants. Oriented to the economy of scarcity and stung by the Depression, the Nearings make a distinction between "bread labor," for subsistence and improvement, and "sufficient leisure to pursue our chosen avocations," including "social pursuits," meaning politics. (Of course, the Nearings do not mean that bread labor is onerous and dull, whereas avocation is pleasant, interesting, and unimportant. Both kinds of work are interesting and worthwhile.) In the turn of history, however, the present emigrants do not think in these terms. The causes are paradoxical. The disgrace of the cities and the degeneration of the high technological culture have been such that just to survive and maintain one's personal integrity has become for the hippies a life's work. In some ways they are, oddly, more like the older Vermonters whom the Nearings regard as pretty shiftless; rural life has again become a way-of-life, now as "counter-culture."

On the other hand, in the amazing affluence of the trillion-dollar GNP and the Welfare State after the New Deal, the issue of making a living, of bread labor, does not have the same psychological and moral force as it did in the Thirties; the young know that they can always subsist anyway. And they would not distinguish between political action and their emigration itself; as a protest against the System, farming as a way-of-life, self-reliance, and improvement of the environment *are* political actions, and they flow into and out of other political actions like going on demonstrations, printing leaflets, harboring draft dodgers, going to jail. In an economic, down-to-earth sense, the Nearings were far more serious than our hippies are; a fairer comparison to the Nearings would be the movement back to the land among some blacks, e.g., the Muslims, to escape the ghetto. But in a religious sense, the hippies are more serious; they are more morally desperate.

Let me put this another way. The critical question for any scheme of subsistence rural reconstruction is its relation to the dominant complex society—how to get the minimum of cash that is necessary and how to have a community and culture that can withstand the urban mores and yet be a useful part of the national whole. The Nearings happened to have a small cash crop of maple sugar, but in their fascinating final chapters, "Rounding out a Livelihood" and "Living in a Community," they tell of their failure in getting the Vermonters to engage in cooperative enterprises so as to compete on the market; or to unite socially and politically, except for the one case of the successful protest against the abolition of the local post office. This failure was partly caused, certainly, by a clash in style between Nearings and neighbors, e.g., it could not help much to speak of "the revolting practice of consuming decaying animal carcasses," not to

mention being teetotal; and, conversely, it must have struck some
of the Vermont ladies as odd that the do-it-yourself Nearings did
not make their own clothes. But mainly, I think, the hang-up
was that the Nearings were proposing a post-urban and post-
industrial schedule to people who were quite content to linger
in the pre-urban and lapse into the pre-industrial whenever they
could. Meantime, however, they could not help but notice, no
doubt to their surprise, that scores and hundreds of city people
came dropping in and hanging around. What did these people
want? They describe with dry humor their methods of coping
with the attractive plague.

But to the hippie farmers, in the present historical dispensa-
tion, this gathering of the tribe is the whole point, the proof and
the fruition. It *is* the counter-culture. Like the old monasteries,
the little farms are way stations on pilgrimages, and they provide havens for runaway kids that are far better than Haight–
Ashbury or the East Village. In the economy of affluence, social
utility is given not by the efficient, cooperative production of
goods—the direction in which the Nearings looked—but in the
provision of services to those starved for life.

In my opinion, this trend indicates the correct path of rural
reconstruction in the next decades. For the foreseeable future,
there will not be economical small cash-farming in this country—
we have not developed the intensive technology, and we have
lost the skills and the character types—although there is always a
market for specialty crops, especially if cooperatively processed
and distributed. But the best hope for the countryside, both as a
source of cash and of social usefulness, is to provide human
services for the cities that the present cities cannot provide as
well, as cheaply, or even at all: a better life for people with welfare checks, places for the primary education of children, havens

for the aged and the harmless "insane" (which usually means simply people who are incompetent in urban conditions), ecological preservation, real vacations instead of the ersatz vacations of summer resorts. Such functions are right at the heart of modern problems, which are city problems, yet they depend on maintaining the difference and integrity of rural life. And they require, needless to say, not mixed-up kids—though these have a place too—but the reliability and scientific common sense of people like Helen and Scott Nearing.

PAUL GOODMAN

New York
April 1970

PREFACE

THIS is a book about a twentieth century pioneering venture in a New England community. Most of the subject matter is derived from twenty years of living in the backwoods of Vermont. The book aims to present a technical, economic, sociological and psychological report on what we tried to do, how we did it, and how well or ill we succeeded in achieving our purposes.

During the deepest part of the Great Depression, in 1932, we moved from New York City to a farm in the Green Mountains. At the outset we thought of the venture as a personal search for a simple, satisfying life on the land, to be devoted to mutual aid and harmlessness, with an ample margin of leisure in which to do personally constructive and creative work. With the passage of time and the accumulation of experience we came to regard our valley in Vermont as a laboratory in which we were testing out certain principles and procedures of more general application and concern.

It was, of course, an individual experience, meeting a special need, at a particular time. When we moved to Vermont we left a society gripped by depression and unemployment, falling a prey to fascism, and on the verge of another world-wide military free-for-all; and entered a pre-industrial, rural community. The society from which we moved had rejected in practice and in principle our pacifism, our vegetarianism and our collectivism. So thorough was this rejection that, holding such views, we could not teach in the schools, write in the press or speak over the radio, and were thus denied our part in public education. Under these circumstances, where could outcasts from a dying social order live frugally and decently, and at the same time have sufficient leisure and energy to assist in the speedy liquidation of the disintegrating society and to help replace it with a more workable social system?

We might have followed the example of many of our compatriots, moved to Paris, Mexico or Paraguay, and allowed the United States to go its chosen way to destruction. We could not accept this alternative because our sense of responsibility as teachers, and as members of the human race, compelled us to do what we could (1) to help our fellow citizens understand the complex and rapidly maturing situation; (2) to assist in building up a psychological and political resistance to the plutocratic military oligarchy that was sweeping into power in North America; (3) to share in salvaging what was still usable from the wreckage of the decaying social order in North America and western Europe; (4) to have a part in formulating the principles and practices of an alternative social system, while meanwhile (5) demonstrating one possibility of living sanely in a troubled world. The ideal answer to this problem seemed to be an independent economy which would require only a small capital outlay, could operate with low overhead costs, would yield a modest living in exchange for half-time work, and therefore would leave half of the year for research, reading, writing and speaking. We decided these tasks could better be performed from a Vermont valley than from a large city or from some point outside the United States. As it turned out, we saved enough time and energy from the bread labor and the association required by our Vermont experiment to take an active though minor part in United States adult education and in the shaping of public opinion, at the same time that we were living what we regarded as a self-respecting, decent, simple life.

We had tried living in several cities, at home and abroad. In varying degrees we met the same obstacles to a simple, quiet life, —complexity, tension, strain, artificiality, and heavy overhead costs. These costs were payable only in cash, which had to be earned under conditions imposed upon one by the city,—for its benefit and advantage. Even if cash income had been of no concern to us, we were convinced that it was virtually impossible to counter city pressures and preserve physical health, mental balance and social sanity through long periods of city dwelling. After careful consideration we decided that we could live a saner, quieter, more worthwhile life in the country than in any urban or suburban center.

We left the city with three objectives in mind. *The first was economic.* We sought to make a depression-free living, as independent as possible of the commodity and labor markets, which could not be interfered with by employers, whether businessmen, politicians or educational administrators. *Our second aim was hygienic.* We wanted to maintain and improve our health. We knew that the pressures of city life were exacting, and we sought a simple basis of well-being where contact with the earth, and home-grown organic food, would play a large part. *Our third objective was social and ethical.* We desired to liberate and dissociate ourselves, as much as possible, from the cruder forms of exploitation: the plunder of the planet; the slavery of man and beast; the slaughter of men in war, and of animals for food.

We were against the accumulation of profit and unearned income by non-producers, and we wanted to make our living with our own hands, yet with time and leisure for avocational pursuits. We wanted to replace regimentation and coercion with respect for life. Instead of exploitation, we wanted a use economy. Simplicity should take the place of multiplicity, complexity and confusion. Instead of the hectic mad rush of busyness we intended a quiet pace, with time to wonder, ponder and observe. We hoped to replace worry, fear and hate with serenity, purpose and at-one-ness.

After twenty years of experience, some of it satisfactory and some of it quite the reverse, we are able to report that:

1. A piece of eroded, depleted mountain land was restored to fertility, and produced fine crops of high quality vegetables, fruits and flowers.

2. A farm economy was conducted successfully without the use of animals or animal products or chemicalized fertilizers.

3. A subsistence homestead was established, paying its own way and yielding a modest but adequate surplus. About three-quarters of the goods and services we consumed were the direct result of our own efforts. Thus we made ourselves independent of the labor market and largely independent of the commodity markets. In short, we had an economic unit which depression could affect but little and which could survive the gradual dissolution of United States economy.

4. A successful small-scale business enterprise was organized and operated, from which wagery was virtually eliminated.

5. Health was maintained at a level upon which we neither saw nor needed a doctor for the two decades.

6. The complexities of city existence were replaced by a fairly simple life pattern.

7. We were able to organize our work time so that six months of bread labor each year gave us six months of leisure, for research, travelling, writing, speaking and teaching.

8. In addition, we kept open house, fed, lodged, and visited

with hundreds of people, who stayed with us for days or weeks, or much longer.

We have not solved the problem of living. Far from it. But our experience convinces us that no family group possessing a normal share of vigor, energy, purpose, imagination and determination need continue to wear the yoke of a competitive, acquisitive, predatory culture. Unless vigilante mobs or the police interfere, the family can live with nature, make themselves a living that will preserve and enhance their efficiency, and give them leisure in which they can do their bit to make the world a better place.

Among the multitudes of friends, acquaintances and strangers who visited us in Vermont, many were so impressed with the project that they wondered whether it would be possible for them to launch a similar undertaking. Some of them discussed the matter with us, and others, who had heard of but had not seen the Vermont place, wrote asking us about it. Interest in the enterprise was stimulated by the publication of several magazine articles commenting on phases of the experiment, and by the appearance, in 1950, of The Maple Sugar Book,[1] in which we wrote down the history and described the technical processes of the industry which provided us with our cash income.

Maple syrup and sugar production was only one phase of an experiment which had other and more important aspects. We suggested some of these in Part III of The Maple Sugar Book, especially in Chapter Ten, "Pioneers, O Pioneers" and Chapter Twelve, "A Life as Well as a Living". In the present volume we are presenting a report on the entire Vermont enterprise, omitting the sugaring details and dealing with the project as a whole. It is our hope that a novice, with the background of experience

[1] Reissued in 1971 by Schocken Books.

recorded in this book, can establish and maintain a health-yielding, harmless, self-contained economy. Such a handbook is needed for the many individuals and families, tied to city jobs and dwellings, who yearn to make their dreams of the good life a reality. May they be encouraged and inspired to attempt such ventures, and may they enjoy them and benefit from them as much as we have done.

Living the Good Life

"Arise, come, hasten, let us abandon the city to merchants, attorneys, brokers, usurers, tax-gatherers, scriveners, doctors, perfumers, butchers, cooks, bakers and tailors, alchemists, painters, mimes, dancers, lute-players, quacks, panderers, thieves, criminals, adulterers, parasites, foreigners, swindlers and jesters, gluttons who with scent alert catch the odor of the market place, for whom that is the only bliss, whose mouths are agape for that alone."

Francesco Petrarch, De Vita Solitaria, *1356*

"My friend, if cause doth wrest thee, ere follie hath much opprest thee: Farre from acquaintance kest thee, Where countrie may digest thee.
Let wood and water request thee, In good corne soile to nest thee,
Where pasture and meade may brest three, And heathsom aire invest thee.
Though envie shall detest thee, Let that no whit molest thee.
Thanke God, that so hath blest thee, And sit downe, Robin, and rest thee."

Thomas Tusser, Five Hundredth Pointes of Good Husbandrie, *1573*

"Would not amoungst roses and jasmin dwel,
Rather than all his spirits choak
With exhalations of dirt and smoak?
And all th' uncleannes which does drown
In pestilentiall clowds a populous town?"

Abraham Cowley, Chertsea, *1666*

"Such is the superiority of rural occupations and pleasures, that commerce, large societies, or crowded cities, may be justly reckoned unnatural. Indeed, the very purpose for which we engage in commerce is, that we may one day be enabled to retire to the country, where alone we picture to ourselves days of solid satisfaction and undisturbed happiness. It is evident that such sentiments are natural to the human mind."

John Loudon, A Treatise on Forming, Improving and Managing Country Residences, *1806*

"I have been seeking through all the valleys to acquire some isolated pasturage which will yet be easily accessible, moderately clement in temperature, pleasantly situated, watered by a stream, and within sound of a torrent or the waves of a lake. I have no wish for a pretentious domain. I prefer to select a convenient site and then build after my own fashion, with the view of locating myself for a time, or perhaps for always. An obscure valley would be for me the sole habitable earth."

E. P. de Senancour, Obermann, *1903*

CHAPTER 1

WE SEARCH FOR THE GOOD LIFE

A change of life—World conditions—Alternative affirmations—Values essential to the good life—Where to live the good life—A setting found in Vermont—From summer folk to all-year-rounders—We buy timberland, and give it away—We hear of mapling—The means of livelihood

MANY a modern worker, dependent on wage or salary, lodged in city flat or closely built-up suburb and held to the daily grind by family demands or other complicating circumstances, has watched for a chance to escape the cramping limitations of his surroundings, to take his life into his own hands and live it in the country, in a decent, simple, kindly way. Caution, consideration for relatives or fear of the unknown have proved formidable obstacles, however. After years of indecision he still hesitates. Can he cope with country life? Can he make a living from the land? Has he the physical strength? Must one be young to start? Where can he learn what he needs to know? Can he build his own house? Can he feed his family from the garden? Must he keep animals? How much will a farm tie him down? Will it be but a new kind of drudgery all over again? These and a thousand

3

other questions flood the mind of the person who considers a
break with city living.

This book is written for just such people. We maintain that
a couple, of any age from twenty to fifty, with a minimum of
health, intelligence and capital, can adapt themselves to country
living, learn its crafts, overcome its difficulties, and build up a
life pattern rich in simple values and productive of personal and
social good.

Changing social conditions during the twenty years that began
in 1910 cost us our professional status and deprived us of our
means of livelihood. Whether we liked it or not we were compelled to adjust to the new situation which war, revolution and
depression had forced upon the western world. Our advancing
age (we were approaching fifty) certainly played some part in
shifting our viewpoint, but of far greater consequence were the
world developments.

Beyond these social pressures our choices were in our own
hands, and their consequences would descend upon our own
heads. We might have stayed on in the city, enduring and re-
gretting what we regarded as essentially unsatisfactory living
conditions, or we might strike out in some other direction, perhaps along a little-used path.

After a careful first-hand survey of developments in Europe
and Asia, as well as in North America, we decided that western
civilization would be unable henceforth to provide an adequate,
stable and secure life even for those who attempted to follow its
directives. If profit accumulation in the hands of the rich and
powerful continued to push the economy toward ever more
catastrophic depressions; if the alternative to depression, under
the existing social system, was the elimination of the unmarket-
able surplus through the construction and uses of ever more

deadly war equipment, it was only a question of time before those who depended upon the system for livelihood and security would find themselves out in the cold or among the missing. In theory we disapproved of a social order activated by greed and functioning through exploitation, acquisition and accumulation. In practice, the outlook for such a social pattern seemed particularly unpromising because of the growing nationalistic sentiments among colonial peoples and the expanding collectivist areas. Added to this, the troubles which increasingly bedeviled western man were most acute at the centers of civilization and were multiplying as the years passed. Under these conditions we decided that we could not remain in the West and live a good life unless we were able to find an alternative to western civilization and its outmoded culture pattern.

Was there an alternative? We looked in three directions for an answer. First we considered and rejected the possibility of living abroad as refugees from what was for us a revolting and increasingly intolerable social situation. Even two decades ago, in the early 1930s, movement was far easier than it is today. In a very real sense, the world lay open before us. Where should we go in search of the good life? We were not seeking to escape. Quite the contrary, we wanted to find a way in which we could put more into life and get more out of it. We were not shirking obligations but looking for an opportunity to take on more worthwhile responsibilities. The chance to help, improve and rebuild was more than an opportunity. As citizens, we regarded it as an assignment. Therefore, we decided not to migrate.

As a second alternative to staying in the urban culture pattern of the West, we checked over the possibilities of life in a cooperative or an intentional community. In the late 1920s the chances of such a solution were few, far between and unpromising. We would have preferred the cooperative or communal alternative, but our experience, inquiries and investigations convinced us that there were none available or functioning into which we could happily and effectively fit.

Finally, we decided on the third alternative, a self-sufficient household economy, in the country, and in the United States, which we would try to make solvent, efficient and satisfying. Having made this decision, our next task was to define our purposes and adjust them to the possibilities of our situation.

We were seeking an affirmation,—a way of conducting ourselves, of looking at the world and taking part in its activities that would provide at least a minimum of those values which we considered essential to the good life. As we saw it, such values must include: simplicity, freedom from anxiety or tension, an opportunity to be useful and to live harmoniously. Simplicity, serenity, utility and harmony are not the only values in life, but they are among the important ideals, objectives and concepts which a seeker after the good life might reasonably expect to develop in a satisfactory natural and social environment. As things stand today, it is not this combination of values, but rather their opposite (that is, complexity, anxiety, waste, ugliness and uproar) which men associate with the urban centers of western civilization.

Our second purpose was to make a living under conditions that would preserve and enlarge joy in workmanship, would give a sense of achievement, thereby promoting integrity and self-respect; would assure a large measure of self-sufficiency and thus make it more difficult for civilization to impose restrictive and coercive economic pressures, and make it easier to guarantee the solvency of the enterprise.

Our third aim was leisure during a considerable portion of each day, month or year, which might be devoted to avocational pursuits free from the exacting demands of bread labor, to satisfying and fruitful association with one's fellows, and to individual and group efforts directed toward social improvement.

Our search for the good life brought us face to face with several immediate questions: Where to live the good life? How to finance the enterprise? And finally there was the central problem of how to live the good life once we had found the place and the economic means.

Where in the United States should we turn? There were countless possibilities. Multitudes were flocking to the sunny southlands, to the Carolinas, Florida, Arizona, New Mexico, California. Others were going north-west. We decided in favor of the north-east, for various reasons. *Aesthetically,* we enjoy the procession of the seasons. In any other part of the country we would have missed the perpetual surprises and delights to which New England weather treats its devotees: the snow piled high in winter and the black and white coloring from December to March; the long lingering spring with its hesitant burgeoning into green; the gorgeous burst of hot summer beauty combined with cool nights; and the crisp snap of autumn with its sudden flare of color in the most beautiful of all the seasons. The land that has four well-defined seasons cannot lack beauty, or pall with monotony. *Physically,* we believe the changing weather cycle is good for health and adds a zest to life. We even enjoy the buffeting that comes with extreme winter cold. *Geographically,* we found New England in closer contact with the Old World, from which we did not wish to sever connections.

We took our time, and during many months looked through the north-eastern states. Finally we settled on Vermont. We liked the thickly forested hills which formed the Green Mountains.

The valleys were cosy, the people unpretentious. Most of the state was open and wild, with little of the suburban or summer vacation atmosphere.

We also picked Vermont for economy's sake. In New York, New Jersey and Eastern Pennsylvania, where we first inquired, land values were high, even in the depression years. By comparison, the prices and costs in Vermont were reasonable.

Where should we go in Vermont? On the map it is a small state compared with some of its big neighbors. From a distance it seemed an easy matter to take a run through the area and check its possibilities, but when we reached the Green Mountains with their steep, curving highways and began to thread our way through the endless mazes of back roads or went on foot from valley to valley, along logging roads and trails which lost themselves in the thickets of underbrush which choke the hillsides, Vermont looked big and baffling. We decided that we needed help. We read the farm ads, gratefully accepted suggestions from friends, and finally fell into the amiable clutches of ex-farmer and present real-estate salesman, L. P. Martin of Newfane, Vermont.

Luke Martin may or may not have been a good farmer, but he was a born realtor. The fulsome descriptions he penned, the small talk and tall tales he traded and the tricks he played must have made him number one man on Beelzebub's roster of real-estaters. Luke boasted that he and his boys sold more Vermont farms than all of the other operators in that area put together. Luke talked steadily, while Gray and Winchester took turns driving the car. After escorting us around the southern part of the state for three consecutive days, they sold us a farm in the town of Winhall. Actually, we bought the first farm they showed us, but between that first view and the purchase we looked at dozens of others. None appealed to us as much as the old Ellonen place, in the Pikes Falls valley which covers part of three townships—Stratton, Winhall and Jamaica. So we went back there on a chill day in the autumn of 1932, and signed an agreement to buy the place.

Its setting and view are lovely. Nestled against a northern slope, the Ellonen place looks up at Stratton Mountain and "The Wilderness", a name applied to the 25,000 acre pulp reserves owned by paper companies. Stratton is a wild, lonely, heavily wooded 4,000 foot mountain, inhabited by 50 or 60 people, where in Daniel Webster's time there had been 1500. "A few score abandoned farms, started in a lean land, held fiercely so long as there was any one to work them, and then left on the hill-sides. Beyond this desolation are woods where the bear and the deer still find peace, and sometimes even the beaver forgets that he is persecuted and dares to build his lodge."[1]

Our new place was a typical run-down farm, with a wooden house in poor repair, a good-sized barn with bad sills and a leaky roof, a Finnish bath house, and 65 acres of land from which the timber had been cut. "Conveniences" consisted of a pump and a black iron sink in the kitchen and a shovel-out backhouse at one end of the woodshed. The place had a plenteous spring of excellent water, a meadow, a swamp or two, and some rough land facing south and stretching perhaps a third of a mile up Pinnacle Mountain, which lay to the east of Stratton. The farm was located on a dirt road seven miles from the Jamaica Post Office and two miles from the hamlet of Bondville. Both villages together had under 600 people in them, and along our ten mile stretch of back-road there were not more than a dozen families.

Peter Ellonen, a Finn, and previous owner of the farm, had

[1] Rudyard Kipling, *Letters of Travel*, N. Y.: Doubleday Page, 1920 p. 11

been killed while working in a feed mill. Most of the children had married and gone away. That left Mrs Peter and her son, Uno, with the farm, which was running down hill and growing up to brush. They were anxious to get out, and sold to us for $300 cash and a Federal Land Bank mortgage of $800.

With the transaction completed, and the deed registered in the name of the new owners, we began to realize what a plunge we had made. The road from New York City to the wilderness was short in miles but far-reaching in social consequences. We were leaping from the economic and social sophistication of a metropolis to a neighborhood in which few of the adults and none of the youngsters had ever visited a large city, in which every house was heated with wood and lighted with kerosene, and in which there was not a single flush toilet. In the first year of our stay we piled the children of several neighbor families in the back of our truck and took them to get their first glimpse of the ocean, to see their first train, to attend their first movie and treated them to their first icecream soda. Coal was an object the children had never known. They handled a piece with interest but could not see how it would burn. They were as removed from modern civilization as if they had been born in some remote Alpine village. We had crossed a wide chasm when we moved from downtown New York to this isolated spot.

We started as "summer folk", who are usually looked on by the native population as socially untouchable and a menace to agriculture. These "foreigners" come with a little or a lot of money, and do not intend to stay long or work much.

In so far as summer residents occupy abandoned land or marginal land unfit for agriculture, they do no great harm. Usually they cultivate little or no land beyond small vegetable and flower gardens. Their pastures go back to wood lots and the

wood lots grow timber without benefit of selective cutting. They
need no income from the land, or they count on its future income.[2] In so far as summer residents occupy productive land,
take it out of use and let it revert to brush, they are a detriment
to the agriculture of the state. Certainly this is true in the more
productive valleys.

Another thing the summer residents do to Vermont agriculture is to put a premium on factory goods and specialties shipped
in from out of state, have them carried in the stores and thus
help to persuade Vermont residents that it is easier and cheaper
to get dollars, exchange them for canned goods sold in the stores,
and abandon long-established gardens in the course of the turn-
over. Thus the state is made less dependent upon its own agriculture and more dependent on dollars, many of which will be
used to buy out-of-state produce.

If this process goes far enough, Vermont will develop a suburban or vacationland economy, built on the dollars of those who
make their income elsewhere and spend part of it during a few
weeks or months of the Vermont summer. Such an economy is
predominately parasitic in terms of production, although income
and expense accounts may be in balance. Carried to its logical
conclusion, it would make Vermonters sell their labor-power to
summer residents, mowing their lawns and doing their laundry,
thus greatly reducing their own economic self-dependence. Such
an economy may attract more cheap dollars to the state, but it
will hardly produce self-reliant men.

Summer people do more than upset Vermont's economy. By
living on their places during the summer and closing them for

[2] "Some rich theorists let the property they purchase lie unoccupied and
unproductive, and speculate upon a full indemnity from the future rise in
value, the more so as they feel no want of the immediate profits." William
Cooper, A *Guide in the Wilderness*, Dublin: Gilbert & Hodges 1810 p. 20

the balance of the year, they turn sections of the State into ghost towns. Neighborhoods, to be meaningful, must have continuity. Part-time towns are parasitic dead towns. "No dwellers, what profiteth house for to stand? What goodnes, unoccupied, bringeth the land?"[3]

The social consequences of turning the countryside into a vacationland are far more sinister than the economic results. What is needed in any community is individuals, householders, villagers and townsmen living together and cooperating day in, day out, year after year, with a sufficient output of useful and beautiful products to pay for what they consume and a bit over. This is solvency in the best social sense. Solvency of this nature is difficult or impossible except in an all-year-round community.

We decided to develop a means of livelihood as soon as possible, so that we could live and work in Vermont through all the year. For a while we shuttled back and forth every two or three months from New York and its New Jersey suburbs to the Vermont farm. Commuting eight or ten times a year across the 216 miles that separated Winhall, Vermont from New York and New Jersey was unsatisfactory, to say the least, and we finally came to the conclusion that our probationary period was over and we would take the plunge. We moved up our belongings in our small truck and passed from part-time summer people to all-year-rounders.

We were not quite sure how newcomers should behave in Vermont, except that we agreed with Captain Basil Hall who wrote in 1829, "I think it should be a rule for persons coming to a new country, always first to follow the customs of that country as closely as possible, reserving their improvements till

[3] Thomas Tusser, *Five Hundredth Pointes of Good Husbandrie*, Lon.: Tottell 1573 p. 11

they get firmly established, and see good reason to apply them."[4] Rather timidly, not wanting to disturb things too much, we cut some poplars near the house and split them up for firewood. It turned out to be the poorest wood on the place. Then we picked the wrong spot and laid out a garden. There was little choice for garden ground on this sixty-five acres, most of which was covered with brush. On the cleared land, flat places were wet or swampy, and dry places were so steep that showers would speedily carry off the topsoil.

The land we picked for gardening did not look too bad in the autumn. It sloped gently to the south and south-west, as a good Vermont garden should, seemed reasonably dry and had a heavy sod deep rooted in black soil. The next spring we learned the reason for the heavy sod and the black soil. A spring opened in the high side of the garden. It dried up in the summer but flowed copiously while the snow was melting and the spring rains were falling. Do what we would, that garden spot was a quagmire until late in the season. We ditched the water around the garden and finally dug a drain across the entire patch, following the slope of the land. Through eternal vigilance and considerable sweat, we coped with the difficulties of drainage, cleared the patch of witch-grass, and in the eight years during which we used that plot, produced some fairly good crops.

Only the well-to-do can go to the country, buy a farm, install a water supply, a bathroom, a refrigerator and electricity, tear down the chicken coop and pig pen, convert the barn into a studio and garage, paint the entire place white, leave on Labor Day and return the second week of the following June. We were not well-to-do, and we had burned our bridges and moved to the wilds on a year-round basis. How were we to keep going?

[4] *Travels in North America*, Phil.: Carey, Lea & Carey, 1829, Vol. I, p. 176

We had thought the matter over and hoped to make our living by the development of a forest and the selective cutting of timber and pulp wood. Forest reproduction is rapid in the Green Mountains and the market for forest products is close at hand. With this in mind, soon after our move we bought a large tract of cut-over land on Pinnacle Mountain, adjoining our place and lying back from the town road. The cost was three dollars an acre. John Tibbets, a Newfane lumberman who owned the tract, had lumbered it off in 1916–19 and had no desire to pay the taxes on the land for twenty or thirty years until another crop of timber was ready for cutting. Cut-over land which does not border on a public road and has no buildings on it can still be bought in this section of Vermont in blocks of a hundred or more acres for under ten dollars an acre.

When lumbermen cut over a tract, they take out only the trees that contain at least one twelve foot log, or the spruce and fir which can be cut into four foot lengths and sold for paper pulp. The land and trees that are left are useless to a lumberman who slashes off timber in a big way, but they offer possibilities as a source of steady cash income for one or two people who are not out to strike it rich, and who are satisfied with a modest cash return.

On the piece of cut-over land, when we bought it, there were many beech, birch and maples with short or crooked or partly rotted trunks, which would not make logs but which would yield a cord or more of firewood per tree. It is possible to convert these cull trees into cordwood, to take out inferior trees such as poplar, soft maple and beech, to cut up the trees which fall in every winter storm, to cull out spruce and fir seedlings into Christmas trees or decorations, to thin young spruce and fir groves for pulp wood and to cut the better trees into logs and cordwood as they mature.[5] Cut-over land, weeded and thinned, and cut selectively as trees become marketable, will yield a man a small, steady income for an indefinite period. Probably he will make less cash on such a project than he could get in wages from a professional lumberman, but he is his own boss and can do the work when it fits best into his own economy.[6]

Such cut-over or "sprout" land had one supreme advantage for people in our position. It required only a small capital outlay and frequently could be bought for an insignificant down payment. To be sure, a lumber company which has slashed the timber from a piece of land and is willing to sell it for a few dollars an acre, will not bother to lay out less than a hundred acres. When Norman Williams tried to buy a piece of cut-over land to the east of Pikes Falls from the Smith Lumber Company, they offered him a hundred acres for $300. He and one of the Smith boys drove four corner stakes around the piece, "by guess and by God". Later we surveyed the piece for them and found that it contained 125 acres. The Smith boys did not worry, however. An extra 25 acres of $3 land was a negligible detail as far as their accounts were concerned. And when Charlie Wellman asked Norm to sell him an acre, Norm obliged, driving stakes at the four corners of a square, 206 by 206 feet. For this acre Charlie paid Norm $3, at a time when a good axe was worth $4.50.

[5] In *The Maple Sugar Book*, Chapters Four and Eleven, we discussed in detail work on the woodlot, and the place of wood cutting in a self-contained rural economy.

[6] "There are few farms in the United States where it is not convenient and profitable to have one or more wood lots attached. They supply the owner with his fuel, which he can prepare at his leisure; they furnish him with timber for buildings, rails, posts and for his occasional demands for implements; they require little attention, and if well managed, yield more or less forage for cattle and sheep. The trees should be kept in a vigorous, growing condition, as the profits are as much enhanced from this cause as any of the cultivated crops." R. L. Allen, *The American Farm Book*, N. Y.: Saxton 1849 p. 295

These rather fantastic figures give an idea of the relatively low price at which cut-over land could be bought and sold in Vermont between 1932 and 1945.

As things turned out, we never got into the timber business, nor did we make use of the Tibbets tract. After paying taxes on it for about eighteen years, we found that it carried an estimated two and a half million board feet of merchantable timber and the lumber barons were after it. The great increase in lumber prices due to the war of 1941–45 had made the Tibbets tract worth more than ten times the amount we paid for it in 1933. Since this increment was due, not to any efforts of ours, but to the growth of the United States in population and wealth, and particularly to participation in war, we made up our minds that we would not profit in any way from the butchering of the trees.

We knew that European towns, in wooded regions, frequently own timber tracts which are forested collectively. These forests are an excellent source of cash income for the towns, and provide enduring and useful monuments which one generation may pass on to its successors. A Vermont State law authorizes towns to own municipal forests, provided that cutting is done under the direction of the State Department of Forestry. So we deeded the entire Tibbets tract to the Town of Winhall in 1951. The next year the Town began cutting one quarter of the area selectively, and under State supervision. If the tract is well handled it should provide the Town with a sizeable income for an indefinite period.[7]

[7] "Though we cannot expect to find many in this Age publick-spirited enough to have such regard to the general Good, as to prefer it before their private Interest; yet the particular Profit that Timber brings to the Owners of it, as well as its Advantage to the Publick, might if it had not caused more Care in propagating of it, have at least prevented those that have had opportunities of experiencing its Advantages, from making that destruction and general spoil that hath everywhere of late been made of Woods." J. Mortimer, *The Whole Art of Husbandry*, Lon.: Mortlock 1712 p. 294

A new possibility had presented itself which turned our minds from lumbering. The first spring after we moved into the Ellonen place, the Hoard boys who lived with their mother, Mercy Hoard, on the next place north of us, burned over their pastures. When they got down in our direction, we noted with alarm that while the two houses were almost half a mile apart, the Hoard land ran to within about a dozen feet of our house and not much farther from our barn. The boys kept the fires under control that day, but the flames came too close for comfort.

We decided to ask Mercy Hoard to sell us a strip of land that would protect our house and barn from future pasture burnings. We found she wanted to move away and she then and there offered us her entire place with its down-at-the-heels buildings, its better than average sugar bush and its decrepit sugarhouse. She wanted a year to cut the 60,000 feet of logs which she estimated were on the place, and after that sold us the farm quite reasonably.

Frank Hoard had been dead for some time when we bought this new place. All of the children except Rodney were grown up and leaving home, and Mercy and the boys had pretty well given up farming. The sugar bush, overgrown with softwood and thick with brush, was being sugared on shares by Floyd Hurd, his wife Zoe, and such of their eleven children as were big enough to lend a hand when sap began to run in the spring. We talked things over with Floyd and Zoe, and continued the original share arrangement. That first year, without raising a finger, we got one-quarter of the syrup crop for the use of the tools and the bush and some fuel. Not knowing what else to do with that amount of syrup, we stored it in gallon cans in an old horse stall in the Ellonen barn. That summer, however, we discovered that maple syrup in Vermont is better than cash. It sells readily and does not depreciate. Here was something on which we had not counted. In a syrup season lasting from four to eight weeks, owning only the maple trees, the sugar house and some poor tools, and doing none of the work, we got enough syrup to pay our taxes and insurance, to provide us with all the syrup we could use through the year, plenty to give away to our friends and to sell. We realized that if we worked at sugaring ourselves, syrup would meet our basic cash requirements.

We were surprised and delighted to learn that here might be the answer to our problem of making a living amid the boulders scattered over the green hills of Vermont. We had been counting on cutting over the woodland as a source of cash income, but there in the barn, before our eyes, stood row upon row of shining cans of maple syrup, all saleable for immediate cash. Up to that moment we had not given a thought to syrup production. We had scarcely noted the sugar houses which dotted the hills all about us, and we had certainly never considered the possibility of our making syrup and sugar. The excellent maple crop in the spring of 1934 opened our eyes to new prospects and put hopes of a solid economic foundation under our Vermont project.

The finding of a spot in Vermont which appealed to our reason, enthusiasms and pocketbooks answered our first question: *where to live the good life*. The possibility of sugaring for a living answered the second question: *how to finance the good life*. Our next job was to determine *the way in which the good life was to be lived*.

"When the sun rises, I go to work,
When the sun goes down, I take my rest,
I dig the well from which I drink,
I farm the soil that yields my food,
I share creation, Kings can do no more."

Ancient Chinese, 2500 B.C.

"O God! methinks it were a happy life,
To be no better than a homely swain,
To set upon a hill, as I do now . . .
So many hours must I tend my flock;
So many hours must I take my rest;
So many hours must I contemplate;
So many hours must I sport myself;
Ah, what a life were this, how sweet! how lovely!"

William Shakespeare, King Henry VI, 1623

"I am retired to Monticello where . . . I enjoy a repose to which I have
been long a stranger. My mornings are devoted to correspondence. From
breakfast to dinner, I am in my shops, my garden, or on horseback among
my farms; from dinner to dark, I give to society and recreation with my
neighbors and my friends; and from candle-light to early bedtime, I read.
My health is perfect, and my strength considerably reinforced by the
activity of the course I pursue; perhaps it is as great as usually falls to the
lot of near 67 years of age. I talk of plows and harrows, of seeding and
harvesting with my neighbors, and of politics too, if they choose, with
as little reserve as the rest of my fellow citizens, and feel, at length, the
blessing of being free to say and do what I please, without being re-
sponsible to any mortal."

Thomas Jefferson, Letter to Kosciusko, Feb. 26, 1810

"No man is born in possession of the art of living, any more than of the
art of agriculture; the one requires to be studied as well as the other,
and a man can no more expect permanent satisfaction from actions per-
formed at random, than he can expect a good crop from seeds sown
without due regard to soil and season . . . Nothing is more conducive
to happiness, than fixing on an end to be gained, and then steadily
pursuing its attainment."

J. C. Loudon, An Encyclopedia of Agriculture, 1825

"There are two ways of living: a man may be casual and simply exist, or
constructively and deliberately try to do something with his life. The
constructive ideas implies constructiveness not only about one's own life,
but about that of society, and the future possibilities of mankind."

Julian Huxley, Essays of a Biologist, 1923

CHAPTER 2

OUR DESIGN FOR LIVING

Our assets—We make a ten year plan—Free of price-profit
—Not out to make money—No I.O.U.'s—Cooperation
wherever possible—Build up a sugar business—Share other
farm products—Keep no animals—We will tear down old
buildings and pick sites for new—We will build of rock,
gathering materials beforehand—The essential gravel pit
and its ramifications—Order heaven's first law—Good tools
will last—Self discipline necessary—Work schedules

THINGS were moving fast—perhaps too fast. We were getting in
deep. Was it too deep? We had acquired three neglected farms
and were starting off at sugaring, of which we knew nothing.
Where were these events leading us? Did the sweeping changes
in our way of life mean commitments and entanglements which
we would regret later on? We had to be wary as well as watchful. Our situation could be summed up in three paragraphs.

We were in the country. We had land. We had all the wood
we could use, for the cutting. We had an adequate supply of
food from the gardens. We had time, a purpose, energy, enough
ingenuity and imagination, a tiny cash income from maple and
a little cash money on hand.

We were on a run-down, run-out farm. We were living in a poorly built wooden house through which the winter winds swept like water through a sieve. We owned a timber tract that would come into its own only in twenty to thirty years. We owned the place next door, another run-down farm, equipped with wretched buildings. Our soil was swampy, rough and rocky, mostly covered with second growth, but there was a small amount of good timber left on it. Our gardens were promising, but the main garden was too low and wet to be really productive.

We were in good health. We were solvent in that we had no debts. We were fairly hopeful of the future, but inexperienced in the ways of subsistence living and somewhat uncertain as to how we should proceed. After due consideration and in the spirit of the times, we drew up a ten year plan.

This plan was not made out of whole cloth, all at once. It was modified by experience, as we went along. It was flexible, but in principle and usually in practice we stuck to it. Suppose we set down the main points which the plan covered when we outlined it in the middle 1930's.

1. *We wish to set up a semi-self-contained household unit, based largely on a use economy, and, as far as possible, independent of the price-profit economy which surrounds us.*

The Great Depression had brought millions of bread-winners face to face with the perils which lurked for those who, in a commodity economy based on wage-paid labor, purchase their livelihood in the open market. The wage and salary workers did not own their own jobs, nor did they have any part in deciding economic policy nor in selecting those who carried policy into effect. The many unemployed in 1932 did not lose their jobs through any fault of their own, yet they found themselves workless, in an economy based on cash payment for the necessaries and decencies. Though their incomes had ceased, their outgo for food, shelter and clothing ate up their accumulated savings and threw them into debt. Since we were proposing to go on living in this profit-price economy, we had to accept its dread implications or find a workable alternative. We saw that alternative in a semi-subsistence livelihood.

We would attempt to carry on this self-subsistent economy by the following steps: (1) Raising as much of our own food as local soil and climatic conditions would permit. (2) Bartering our products for those which we could not or did not produce. (3) Using wood for fuel and cutting it ourselves. (4) Putting up our own buildings with stone and wood from the place, doing the work ourselves. (5) Making such implements as sleds, drays, stone-boats, gravel screens, ladders. (6) Holding down to the barest minimum the number of implements, tools, gadgets and machines which we might buy from the assembly lines of big business.[1] (7) If we had to have such machines for a few hours or days in a year (plough, tractor, rototiller, bull-dozer, chain-saw), we would rent or trade them from local people instead of buying and owning them.

2. *We have no intention of making money, nor do we seek*

[1] All through the years in Vermont we had one expensive, indispensable machine, a half-ton pick-up truck. The first one was a Dodge; later came Fords and Chevrolets, until we got a Jeep, which proved incomparably superior to the others because of its four-wheel drive. If we had done our driving on concrete highways, the four-wheel mechanism would have been superfluous, but on back roads, across fields and through the woods, up and down hills, in mud, snow, slush and on ice, the four-wheel drive paid for its extra cost in one season. Occasionally there might be something, logs, for example, which we could not handle in a pick-up with a body 48 inches wide by 78 inches long, though we did rig up a device that enabled us to carry easily and in quantity, standard iron pipe lengths 21 feet long and even longer poles. The pick-up handled lumber, gravel, stone, lime, cement, topsoil, cord wood and sugar wood, freight and express. It also delivered our sugar products, and carried us many thousand miles each year

wages or profits. Rather we aim to earn a livelihood, as far as possible on a use economy basis. When enough bread labor has been performed to secure the year's living, we will stop earning until the next crop season.

Ideas of "making money" or "getting rich" have given people a perverted view of economic principles. The object of economic effort is not money, but livelihood. Money cannot feed, clothe or shelter. Money is a medium of exchange,—a means of securing the items that make up livelihood. It is the necessaries and decencies which are important, not the money which may be exchanged for them. And money must be paid for, like anything else. Robert Louis Stevenson wrote in *Men and Books*, "Money is a commodity to be bought or not to be bought, a luxury in which we may either indulge or stint ourselves, like any other. And there are many luxuries that we may legitimately prefer to it, such as a grateful conscience, a country life, or the woman of our inclination."[2]

People brought up in a money economy are taught to believe in the importance of getting and keeping money. Time and again folk told us, "You can't afford to make syrup. You won't make any money that way." One year a neighbor, Harold Field, kept a careful record of the labor he put in during the syrup season and of the sale price of his product, and figured that he got only 67 cents an hour for his time. In view of these figures, the next year he did not tap out because sugaring paid less than wage labor. But, during that syrup season he found no chance to work for wages, so he didn't even make the 67 cents an hour.

Our attitude was quite different. We kept careful cost figures, but we never used them to determine whether we should or should not make syrup. We tapped our trees as each sap season

[2] Lon.: Chatto & Windus 1888 p. 143

came along. Our figures showed us what the syrup had cost. When the season was over and the syrup on hand, we wrote to various correspondents in California or Florida, told them what our syrup had cost, and exchanged our product for equal value of their citrus, walnuts, olive oil or raisins. As a result of these transactions, we laid in a supply of items at no cash outlay, which we could not ourselves produce. Our livelihood base was broadened as the result of our efforts in the sugar bush and the sap house.

We also sold our syrup and sugar on the open market. In selling anything, we tried to determine exact costs and set our prices not in terms of what the traffic would bear but in terms of the costs,—figuring in our own time at going day wages.

Just as each year we estimated the amount of garden produce needed for our food, so we tried to foresee the money required to meet our cash obligations. When we had the estimated needs, we raised no more crops and made no more money for that period. In a word, we were trying to make a livelihood, and once our needs in this direction were covered, we turned our efforts in other directions,—toward social activities, toward avocations such as reading, writing, music making, toward repairs or replacements of our equipment.

3. *All of our operations will be kept on a cash and carry basis. No bank loans. No slavery to interest on mortgages, notes and I.O.U's.*

Under any economy, people who rent out money live on easy street. Whether as individuals or banking establishments, they lend money, take security and live on a rich harvest of interest and the proceeds of forced sales. The money lenders are able to enjoy comfort and luxury, without doing any productive labor. It is the borrowing producers who pay the interest or lose their

property. Farmers and home owners by the thousands lost everything they had during the Great Depression because they could
not meet interest payments. We decided to buy for cash or not
at all.

4. *We will make our cash crop from maple syrup and will work
out a cooperative arrangement wherever possible.* We made a
cooperative agreement with Floyd Hurd and his family under
which we would work together and divide the syrup crop in
proportion to land and tools owned and the work done by each
party. We began this arrangement in 1935 and continued it for
six years with the Hurds, later carrying it on with other people.

5. *We will put syrup production on an efficient basis, replace
the old Hoard sugarhouse with a modern building and equip it
with new tools.* We did this in 1935, we building the new sugarhouse and the Hurds buying a large new evaporator. We also
decided to convert part of our syrup crop into maple sugar, for
which there was a ready sale. The complete story of this effort
has been told in detail in *The Maple Sugar Book.*

6. *So long as the income from the sale of maple syrup and sugar
covers our needs we will not sell anything else from the place.
Any garden or other surpluses will be shared with neighbors and
friends in terms of their needs.*

This latter practice was carried out generally in the valley. Rix
Knight had extra pear trees. In a good season he distributed
bushels to any of us who had no pears. Jack Lightfoot let us
pick his spare apples and let others cut Christmas greens, free of
charge. We brought firewood to those who needed it, and many
garden products. Our chief delight was growing, picking and
giving away sweet peas. We grew these in profusion,—double
rows 60 to 100 feet long, each year. Whenever taking a trip to
town in blooming season (July to frost of late September) we

filled baskets and basins with dozens of bunches and gave them out during the day to friends and strangers alike. Grocers, dentist friends, gas station attendants, utter strangers on the street,— all were the delighted recipients of the fragrant blossoms. One woman, after endeavoring to pay for a large bunch, was heard to go off muttering, "I've lived too near New York too long to understand such practices."

7. *We will keep no animals.* Almost without exception, Vermont farmers have animals, often in considerable variety. We do not eat animals, or their products, and do not exploit them. We thus escape the servitude and dependence which tie both farmer and animal together. The old proverb "No man is free who has a servant" could well read "No man is free who has an animal."

Animal husbandry on a New England farm involves building and maintaining not only sheds but barns and the necessary fences, and also the cutting or buying of hay. Into this enterprise goes a large slice of the farmer's time. Farm draft animals work occasionally but eat regularly. Many of them eat more than they produce and thus are involuntary parasites. All animals stray at times, even with the best of fences, and like all runaway slaves, must be followed and brought back to servitude. The owners of horses, cattle, pigs and chickens wait on them regularly, as agrarian chamber maids, feeding, tending them and cleaning up after them. Bernard Shaw has said: "Millions of men, from the shepherd to the butcher, become mere valets of animals while the animals live, and their executioners afterwards."

We believe that all life is to be respected—non-human as well as human. Therefore, for sport we neither hunt nor fish, nor do we feed on animals. Furthermore, we prefer, in our respect for life, not to enslave or exploit our fellow creatures. Widespread and unwarranted exploitation of domestic animals includes rob-

bing them of their milk or their eggs as well as harnessing them
to labor for man. Domestic animals, whether cows, horses, goats,
chickens, dogs or cats are slaves. Humans have the power of life
or death over them. Men buy them, own them, sell them, work
them, abuse and torture them and have no compunctions against
killing and eating them. They compel animals to serve them in
multitudinous ways. If the animals resist, rebel or grow old, they
are sent to the butcher or else are shot out of hand.

Cats and dogs live dependent subservient lives under the table
tops of humans. Domestic pets kill and drive away wild creatures, whose independent, self-respecting lives seem far more
admirable than those of docile, dish-fed retainers. We enjoy the
wild creatures, and on the whole think they are more lithe, beautiful and healthy than the run of cats and dogs, although some
of our best friends in Vermont have been canine and feline
neighbors.

While remaining friends with all kinds of animals, we preferred to be free from dependents and dependence. Many a
farmer, grown accustomed to his animal-tending chores and to
raising food for animals instead of for himself, could thus find his
worktime cut in half.

8. *We will not waste time making over old buildings. We will
use them as long as necessary, repair them if we must, but in
general we realise they are on the skids. If they have no function,
we will tear them down at the first opportunity. Only if they are
useful and necessary, will we replace them.*

We wanted a fireplace in the Ellonen house. The only practicable way to get it was to add a room; there was no other possible space. So we built a 12 x 12 foot stone-walled addition, with
a stone fireplace, a stone floor and pine-panelled walls. With that
exception, we made only urgently necessary repairs to the old

Ellonen buildings, although we lived in the house for nine years before we moved into new quarters.

Some of our friends and neighbors cry out in protest: "But the lines on these old houses!" Our answer is simple, and in three parts. (1) If we are worth a snap of the fingers, we can build with lines as good or better than our great-grandfathers. If we cannot, we do not deserve to live in a well-designed house. (2) The refurbishing of an old building will often cost as much, and sometimes more, in time and money than the construction of a new one.[3] (3) When you get all through with the old building you still have an old framework, which means old and often rotten sills, studs, plates, floor joists and rafters. Corners or lines may never be square or true, and the style and planning are not really custom-fitted to the modern occupant. "He that alters an old house is as tied as a translator to the original, and is confined to the fancy of the first builder."[4]

A dozen times, since we moved to Vermont, we have watched relatives and friends remodel old buildings. We think that the three points in the preceding paragraph applied in every instance.

9. *We will pick out the sites for a permanent house and other necessary buildings, and for gardens which can be terraced for drainage during wet seasons and can be irrigated in dry spells.* Chapter Three "Building a Stone House" and Chapter Four "Our Good Earth" give details of the way we put this ninth proposition into practice.

10. *We will build of natural stone and rock. This can be done*

---

[3] "I may remark here, in way of warning to those who undertake the renovation of slatternly country places with exuberant spirits, that it is a task which often seems easier than it proves." D. G. Mitchell, *My Farm of Edgewood,* N.Y.: Scribner 1863 p. 57

[4] Thomas Fuller, *The Holy State and the Profane State,* Cambridge: Daniel 1632 p. 166

most efficiently by gathering the materials long beforehand. We will sort all stone that we have to move, establish piles for wall stones, corner stones, chimney stones, floor stones, terrace stones and fireplace stones to prepare for the years when we can build.

From the birth of our idea of building a stone house we started collecting these rocks.[5] From roadsides, from our garden, gravel pit, old stone walls, on walks in the woods, all over the countryside we kept our eyes open for well-shaped rocks, of any cartable size. We followed old Thomas Tusser's advice: "Come home from land, with stone in hand", said he.[6] "Where stones be too manie, annoieng thy land, Make servant come home with a stone in his hand. By daily so dooing, have plentie yee shall, Both handsome for paving and good for a wall."[7] Some desirable stone we even trucked in from out-of-state. Neighbors became interested, and turning up good rock with the plow or the pick, contributed them to our growing piles.

We set aside a convenient locality, out of the way of building or hauling, but handy to our site. We put up rough sign-boards labelled "Corner", for stones having one 90° angle; "Blue Ribbon", for those having a good flat face; "Floor", for thin, large rocks having a smooth flat surface; "Chimney", for regular blocks, with well-set corners if possible; and "Uglies", for just plain stone, of odd sizes and shapes, which could be used for foundations or for fillers. Stone gathering became a real preoccupation on our

---

[5] "A great part of the cost of a stone building is the expense of collecting the materials . . . If the materials should be collected in winter, or at any leisure time, and be handy to the spot, it is presumed that the cost of a neat and handsome house would not exceed much, if any, the expense of a wooden building, when the timber and the boards are to be purchased and carted from some distance." J. M. Gourgas, in *The New England Farmer*, April 4, 1832, p. 298

[6] *Five Hundred Pointes of Good Husbandrie*, Lon.: Tottell 1573 p. 96

[7] *Ibid.*, p. 99

walks or drives, and it was a rare day when we did not come back "with stone in hand."

11. *First among the new buildings to be erected in our construction program will be a lumber shed where our green lumber can be stored and dried under the best conditions. This will give us air-dried lumber when we come to build.* As it turned out, our supply of lumber put in the shed in 1933–36, provided us during the years from 1938–43 (when we did most of our building), with $25 lumber at a time when the same lumber, green at the mill, was hard to get at $125 per thousand feet.

12. *Since building with concrete requires sand and gravel, we will need a dependable source of good gravel and sand.* This was a must! So we set out in 1934 in search of a satisfactory gravel pit.

We were not alone in our search for gravel. We lived on a dirt road, which the town had to patch continually, repair and rebuild with gravel. The town roadmen told us that there was only one good gravel pit within easy hauling distance. They had made repeated tests elsewhere in the valley, they said, but without success. The available pit belonged to an estate administered by Dr. Heflon of Jamaica. It was in this pit that the roadmen got their supply. For a time we hauled sand and gravel from that pit. Then the estate was sold to some New Yorkers who said they did not want any gravel trucks running through their front yard, and they forbid entrance. The closing of this pit meant hauling gravel from the other side of the mountain. We took this in our stride and began getting it from miles away, but the material was very fine and mixed with quicksand and clay, both of which spoil concrete.

While we were puzzling over this problem, Charlie White happened to stop us one day on a trip to Jamaica. "You don't want

to buy a piece of land up your way?" he asked. We said we had
plenty, but as an afterthought inquired where it was. It turned
out to be a 13 acre tract adjoining the place on which the New
York owners had closed the gravel pit. We looked it over, tested
it in several places, decided that it contained good gravel and
asked the owner, Sadie Clayton, how much she wanted for it.
She said her price was $100. "But", she said, "Merrill Stark has
put down $25 on the place and he was going to buy it. His option
has run out and he hasn't any money. I don't want to pay taxes
on it, so I'm going to sell it."

Here was a bear-trap. Merrill Stark, of the famous Vermont
Stark family, lived at Pikes Falls, two miles south of us. There
were the makings of a neighborhood feud here if we bought the
land he wanted. How could we get it amicably?

After discussion, we made Sadie Clayton this offer: We will
give you a check for $100 drawn to you, a check for $25 drawn
to Merrill Stark, and we will pay the back taxes on the tract,
which amounted to about $10. Sadie Clayton accepted, Merrill
Stark got back his $25 and was friendly and neighborly to us
until his death several years later, and we got a badly needed
gravel pit.

Of course we had no use for 12 acres of gravel. One acre was
enough. So we opened up a pit at a place that seemed handiest to
the road, staked off something less than two acres at this end of
the tract and divided the remainder of the land into two pieces.
On one of these we built a small log cabin, an experiment for
us in this kind of building, and sold it for $600. We learned a
lot in the building of it, and the principal lesson was not to build
again of logs.[8] On the other piece of land we built a four room,

[8] "If I were commencing life again in the woods, I would not build anything
of logs except a shanty or a pig-sty; for experience has plainly told me that

one-story stone building with a stone springhouse at the back, which we sold for $2,000. Into the latter building, which was located about 100 yards from the gravel pit, went the rocks which were coming in large quantities from the stone piles remaining after we had taken out sand and gravel. We built stone fireplaces and chimneys into both houses.

We look upon profits and the profit system as iniquitous. Therefore we kept careful expense accounts on these two houses, allowed ourselves day wages for the time we put in on them, added land costs, material and building costs, and thus arrived at a profit-free selling price. The building and sale of the two houses brought us much experience and a small amount of capital which we promptly invested in our other building projects.

Gravel pit yields included sods and topsoil with which we built up our terraced gardens and compost piles; subsoil and boulders which we used for fill on construction jobs; stone and sand and gravel which went into walls, floors and chimneys. We kept the top of the pit skinned back to reduce the likelihood of organic matter getting into the underlying clean gravel and sand. We constructed a rough gravel screen which separated pit material into three grades—sand, gravel up to 1½ inches in diameter, and small stones. These stones were ideal for road work. They solidified mudholes and made hard wheel tracks. In eighteen years, beside a small amount of material used by the town, and some

---

log buildings are the dirtiest, most inconvenient, and the dearest, when everything is taken into consideration. As soon as the settler is ready to build, let him put up a good frame, roughcast, or stone house, if he can possibly raise the means, as stone, timber, and lime cost nothing but the labour of collecting and carrying the materials. When I say that they 'cost nothing', I mean that no cash is required for these articles, as they can be prepared by the exertion of the family." Samuel Strickland, 27 *Years in Canada West*, Lon.: Bentley 1853 Vol. I. pp. 170-1

given to friends and neighbors, we removed 5,050 pick-up truck loads of material from the gravel pit.

During the course of years we took out enough good earth to enlarge the truck-garden, enough non-building rocks and even roots and other coarse material to fill a swamp so that we could drive around the sugarhouse woodshed, and enough subsoil and rough stones to build and add to many roads round the place. All material was used, from loam down through the various strata to fine gravel. The fill behind the sugarhouse woodshed, for instance, was a deep drop that could absorb anything up to four feet in diameter.

Projects of this type, rushed to completion in a few months, would have involved a heavy outlay of time and would have led to delay in the fulfillment of other more essential features of our over-all plan. Actually, the third and final unit of the truck garden was completed and put into full production eleven years after the first unit of the truck garden was begun. When finished, it was about 75 feet long by 28 feet wide. It was divided into three units or terraces by concrete and stone retaining walls. Into this garden we put about 300 truck loads of soil. We built the first unit immediately as an urgent project, because we needed the food supply. After that, we built the truck garden only as we had available materials. The lower side of the garden consisted of a fill which in some places was six feet deep. Into such a deep fill we could put almost any type of subsoil. As we approached the garden level, however, we used only first grade topsoil.

We aimed never to move stones, earth or any material more than once—directly to its final resting place. We had many projects going on at the same time, in various stages of completion. Thus, the finishing of these successive units was a by-product of the wastes from other projects. In a sense they cost us nothing, because it was necessary in any case to move these materials. In another sense they were a dividend, because had we moved these superfluous materials and dumped them just anywhere, we would have ended up with a littered, unsightly landscape, whereas with our procedure, each load of material from foundation or gravel pit was ticketed in advance to a specific destination and for a specific purpose. In a very real sense the truck garden was not built, it grew, over a decade, as a part of a general plan aimed toward a place for everything (including wastes), and everything to its place.

These twelve points were the essentials of our ten year plan,— the items in our card catalog. They made up the Constitution of our household organization. We also drew up by-laws of household procedure, the first of which called for order.

We were planning a functioning homestead, not a business; nevertheless we tried to be as systematic as though we were handling a large-scale economic project. Our card index of activities had a place for "jobs to be done", divided into "clear weather jobs" and "rainy day jobs", for "construction planned", and for "finished projects". Each project had its cost cards with records of materials used and money outlay for specific purposes. Separate loose-leaf books for gardening and sugaring contained the plans, current activity reports and records from previous years.

Under "Winter Evenings" in *The Farmer's Calendar*,[9] Arthur Young advises the farmer thus: "Every work for the next day is to be arranged, whether for fine or rainy weather, and the farm-books to be made up for the transactions of the past day. Besides these, he should have another book, for miscellaneous observa-

[9] Lon.: Phillips 1805 pp. 51-2

tions, queries, speculations, and calculations, for turning and comparing different ways of effecting the same object . . . Loose pieces of paper are generally lost after a time, so that when a man wants to turn to them to examine a subject formerly estimated or discussed, he loses more time in searching for a memorandum, than would be sufficient for making half a dozen new ones; but if such matters are entered in a book, he easily finds what he wants, and his knowledge will be in a much clearer progression, by recurring to former ideas and experience."

We tackled our practical problems one by one, as we reached them. In each case we followed a pattern which began with a survey of the situation, continued with a discussion or series of discussions which led to a decision, often written down in memorandum, black on white. The decision was elaborated into a plan, also written out and often revised. Finally the plan was checked and coordinated with our ten year plan, adopted as a project and fitted into the work schedule.[10]

Some of our readers will feel that such a life pattern is over-organized. They would not wish to plan their activities so completely. After having tried it out, day after day, and year after year, we know it is the way to get things done. Two people can accomplish much in a day or a month or a year if they have defined objectives, agreed plans, if they work on the program systematically and conscientiously, giving as much attention to details as to the over-all plan.

Take an illustration from the handling and conditioning of

[10] Native Vermonters are wary of lawyers and they shy off at the sight of legal documents. Only under pressure will they put their names on a "paper". On several occasions, when considerable detail was involved, as in the division of maple syrup among those cooperating in its production, we talked the matter over, made notes of the points on which we agreed, typed the notes with carbons and handed around copies of the memorandum. In such cases no one signed, but the memorandum was a useful record.

tools. We had a place for each tool. Shovels, hoes, rakes and bars were in racks on the right as we entered the tool shed. There were as many holes in the racks as there were tools. No one ever had to hunt for a shovel or a hoe. If one was missing, a glance showed its absence and we searched until we located it. If we could not find it, we replaced it. Actually, with this system, we almost never lost a tool.

After each job which was completed in less than a working day, the tools went back into their places. At the end of each day's work we followed the same procedure. Consequently, tools which were not in place were in actual use and tools not in use were in place. We tried to follow this practice even though a tool was used on several jobs in the course of one working day. To further classify and locate tools, we painted a bright stripe of color on their handles. If left in the grass or on top of a job they were easy to see and identify.

Our neighbors, knowing we were well supplied, borrowed many tools. Of these, we tried to keep duplicates as otherwise we were often left short-tooled. Gervase Markham advocated this practice in 1616 in his *Countrey Farme*.[11] "He must have Tooles and Instruments twice so manie in store as he useth to have Workmen, to the end they need not to borrow anything of their neighbours, for otherwise hee shall lose more in dayes workes not fulfilled than would pay for the buying of his yron Tooles."

Ordinarily, capital goods should last a lifetime. Our cement mixer, for instance, bought new in 1933 for $20 was still doing good work when we passed it on to Herbert Leader twenty years later. We cleaned it up after each job and oiled it and housed it over the winter. It was a hand mixer, and many a visitor told us

[11] Lon.: Adam Flip p. 22

how we could hook it up with a gas engine or an electric motor. We continued to operate it by hand, however, and the capital outlay of twenty dollars for the mixer (minus its considerable value in 1953) spread over twenty years, came to less than one dollar per year.

Incidentally, our refusal to convert our hand mixer into a power tool had several noteworthy results. (1) We saved the time, labor, capital outlay, upkeep and replacement costs incident to the operation of all power tools. (2) We saved the outlay for gasoline or electricity. (3) We avoided the anxiety, tension, frustration and loss of time caused by mechanical breakdowns. Advocates of mechanization do not like to face the fact that a machine gets tired, gets sick and dies during its life cycle, and that a machine tender must be prepared to meet these emergencies in the life of a machine in much the same way that he must meet them in the life cycle of a domestic animal such as a horse or of any other slave. (4) Turning the mixer with first one hand and then the other, we got balanced muscle-building, invigorating, rejuvenating physical exercise in the fresh air, under the open sky,—one important ingredient in the maintenance of good health. (5) We had the satisfaction of participating directly in the project, instead of wet-nursing a machine and inhaling its oil fumes and carbon monoxide.

At this point some reader may ask us two quite reasonable questions. First, if we seek to avoid machinery, why not use a shovel instead of a hand mixer? Our reply is that much of the time we did. All of our pointing mixtures were made by hand. Also on all small jobs we mixed concrete in a steel wheelbarrow. It is easier to lug a wheelbarrow to a job than it is to lug a mixer. Furthermore, a barrow can be washed up in a quarter or a fifth of the time that it takes to wash up a mixer.

The second question might be "If you were building Hoover Dam, would you mix concrete in a wheelbarrow?" Our answer: Probably not. The machine has its function, especially on gigantic undertakings. Our project was not gigantic, but minute. We were busy setting up and maintaining a self-sufficient household. In such an enterprise machine tools are, on the whole, a liability rather than an asset.

Mankind has worked for ages with hand implements. Machine tools are a novelty, recently introduced into the realm of human experience. There can be no question but that machines have more power than humans. Also there can be no question but that they have watered down or annihilated many of the most ancient, most fascinating and creative human skills, broken up established institutions, pushed masses of "hands" into factories and herded droves of anonymous footloose wanderers from urban slum to urban slum. Only the historian of the future will be able to assess the net effect of the machine age on human character and on man's joy in being and his will to live.

We were saying that the cost of capital goods can be spread over a great period of time when we allowed ourselves to digress into a discussion growing out of a reference to our faithful and long-suffering cement mixer. We continue with our argument.

The surveyor's level and compass transit which we used in our grading and building we inherited from a grandfather. Both were made by Stackpole and Brother (long-since deceased) in the middle of the nineteenth century. Both sufficed for our simple engineering needs. Many of our hammers, saws, planes, shaves and metal tools had been well cared for and had served the needs of two and three generations. Had this equipment been left, even for brief periods, out in the weather, its life would have been shortened. Had it remained outside through the late fall and winter, it would have been soon unfit for use.[12]

We argued this point, to little purpose, with several of our neighbors. Invariably they replied that it was easier to leave the tools "handy to the field" than it was to bring them in. Many of these men had shed room and simply failed to use it.

In some ways exposure to the weather is more disastrous for the metal on tools than for the wood. Wood also suffers, however. One summer we had a job that involved handling clay in a $35 rubber-tired contractor's wheelbarrow. At the end of each day's work we washed the barrow with a hose and put it under cover for the night. Although the wooden handles of the barrow had been painted, within a month they showed serious deterioration as a result of repeated wetting and drying. We countered with generous doses of old engine-oil and saved the day.[13]

In our tool shed, at the right side of the shovel rack, hung two pieces of burlap sacking on nails. As each shovel came from a job it was wiped clean and dry with the burlap. In the winter each shovel got a coat of oil, applied in half a minute with a rejected paint brush. The shovels were never rusty, therefore clay and loam did not stick to them, nor did they require banging and scraping on the job. Clean tools do more work with less labor.

[12] "A farmer, by the nature of things, ought to be a man of strict economy. His aim ought to be habitually to prevent waste, in anything, and in all things. After he has paid $70 for his ox wagon, and $45 for the cart, they should not be left exposed to the ardent sun, nor to the rain, but carefully housed under sheds, when not in use. Plough and tools should be secured in the same way." J. M. Gourgas, in New England Farmer, 1/25/1828 p. 209

[13] Tool handles and other wooden parts may be painted to advantage, but the paint wears off speedily. A more effective treatment is to brush on a coat of engine oil whenever openings begin to show between the grains of the wood. A bit of fine dust, rubbed on when the oil is applied, gives the handle a pleasantly smooth surface and seals the wood pores against moisture penetration.

Axes were in a compartment next to the shovels. Each night after work, the axes went into their places. If they were dull, they were sharpened. There is more difference on a job between a dull axe and a sharp axe than there is between night and day.

With care, capital costs can be held down and capital goods can be made to last so long that the annual outlay for upkeep and replacement is reduced close to zero. Bought new, they require considerable cash expenditure, especially if purchased on installments and left out in the weather or turned over to children for playthings.

During the autumn months, as we gave the gravel pit a final once-over, inspected the sap pipelines, swept out the tool shed, sowed rye in the big garden, stored the root vegetables and the apples, and put the snow-stakes along the road and beside the culverts, we asked ourselves: "Well, what is our project for next year?" In the course of weeks or months, we talked over various possibilities, decided between them, put our decisions on paper, drew our plans, filed them in the appropriate place and were ready well ahead of time to start on them when spring came. If we found we were short of lumber for some building operation, we cut logs during the winter, put them on skids and sent them to the mill as soon as roads hardened up in the spring. We aimed to keep our lumber shed full of miscellaneous pieces for odd jobs or big projects. Our woodsheds too were filled ahead of time. We considered dry wood under cover better than money in the bank. Our inventories for the sugar business were kept well filled so that needs were anticipated and crises due to lack of essential materials were avoided. When we had money, we put it into building. If we could not finish a building one year, we stopped at a planned point and finished it the next year.

In order to carry out our various plans we had to use a certain amount of self-discipline, and expected it of those who lived with us. There were three kinds of work to be done on the farm: (1) household routine: the getting of meals, washing up, and keeping the house clean; (2) organized homestead activities: bread labor such as gardening, wood-cutting, repairs, replacements, capital construction on plant, buildings and equipment; and (3) work on the cash crop or crops.

Amongst the various people who shared our life at Forest Farm were, first, those who dropped in for a day or two. These we regarded as guests and did not try to fit them into the pattern of the place, except to let them help prepare meals and wash up.

Second, were those who stayed over a week. These we dubbed transients, and let them help with organized homestead activities for half of their time.

Last, came the permanent residents. They helped in labor categories *one* and *two*, shared all food produced on the place and could build living quarters for themselves,—we providing the building site, materials and help with plans and labor. Initiative and responsibility rested with the permanent resident. When they wished to participate in the production of the cash crop, they shared on an agreed cooperative basis.

All guests and transients were put up in our guesthouse and ate their meals with us. We aimed to make the mealtime a social event. Friends staying with us or visitors who happened to drop in knew that meals were social occasions. Whoever was present when a meal was announced—be it customer, stranger or friend—was invited to breakfast, lunch or supper. Frequently it was necessary to set a second table in our combination kitchen-dining-room.

Each day was divided into two main blocks of time—four morning hours and four afternoon hours. At breakfast time on week-days we first looked at the weather, then asked "How shall we arrange the day?" Then by agreement we decided which of these blocks of time should be devoted to bread labor and which to personally determined activities. Of necessity the weather was the primary factor in making the decision.

Suppose that the morning was assigned for bread labor. We then agreed upon the tasks that each member of the group should take on—in the garden, in the woods, on construction, in the shop, at sugarmaking or packing. If one's bread labor was performed in the morning, the afternoon automatically became personally directed. One might read, write, sit in the sun, walk in the woods, play music, go to town. We earned our four hours of leisure by our four hours of labor.

There is another very important point to remember about our projects. We were not in a hurry, except occasionally when it threatened to shower or when sap buckets were running over, or on special Christmas rush orders. All such emergencies we tried to anticipate as much as possible, in order to avoid haste, which according to the old saying, results in waste. We took our time, every day, every month, every year. We had our work, did it and enjoyed it. We had our leisure, used it and enjoyed that. During the hours of bread labor we worked and worked hard. We have never worked harder and have never enjoyed work more, because, with rare exceptions, the work was significant, self-directed, constructive and therefore interesting.[14]

There was no boss. No one pushed anyone else around. When Hank Mayer worked with us, he came from a big construction job. After the first day, he said skeptically, "I don't see how you get anything done around here. Nobody is yelling at anyone else."

[14] "What is the good of life if its chief element, and that which must always be its chief element, is odious? No, the only true economy is to arrange so that your daily labour shall be itself a joy." Edward Carpenter, *Non-Governmental Society*, Lon.: Fifield 1911 p. 15

Each was expected to contribute according to his energy and ability and for the most part, each did. There was little idling or shirking. Occasionally our difficulty was not to get people to work, but to keep them from it. The garden was a special temptation. There is always something to do in a garden. After a morning of planting or thinning, there would be some ragged edges that were not cleaned up by noon. It was so easy to slip down to the garden after lunch, intending to plant just one more row or put in those few tomato stakes. Before you knew it, half the afternoon was gone and still the garden beckoned.

When Jacob Apsel came to stay with us, he was a bit restless and uncertain as to his future and what he wanted to do. His nervousness found release in working. So day after day he would take on a morning of bread labor, and then after lunch go on with an afternoon of the same. It was a month or six weeks before we could persuade him to put his free half-day into reading or some other activity not associated with the production of our livelihood. After a time he caught on and enjoyed his four hours leisure as much as his four hours of bread labor. Jacob learned the lesson that to get things done, leisure is often as important, or, in case a person is over-tense, more important than work.

Each person on our project took vacations—blocks of time ranging from weeks to months, which were set off against equal periods of bread-labor time. We talked these matters over well in advance, arranging the vacation schedules in a way that made sense in terms of work urgency on one side and personal preference on the other. Our aim was to get a year's livelihood in return for half a year of bread labor. We were quite flexible in arranging the details. Occasionally we would work steadily for months and then take off months away from work.

On Sundays we varied our schedule by having no schedule and by doing no regular bread-labor. Usually there was a period of music Sunday morning and often a group discussion Sunday evenings. Other evenings there was a period of reading aloud by someone while the others cracked nuts, shelled beans or did some personal chore like darning or knitting. We adhered generally to this daily and weekly routine, but not fanatically. However, unless there was a good and sufficient reason, we did not depart from it.

Need we say that our Vermont neighbors were appalled by such a planned and organized life? They were accustomed to a go as you-please existence. They usually ate at noon, but that was the one fixed point in the day unless someone was working out on a regular job and had to report at a specified hour. They got up and went to work, or did not go to work, as a result of accident or whim. If someone came along and wanted to visit, they would turn from almost any job and chat, sometimes for hours. When they did decide to work, they let inclination determine the object of their efforts. When they got through with a tool, they dropped it. When they wanted it again, sometimes half the day was wasted in search. If the morning looked like rain or snow, they "sat on their heels" in the local vernacular. They naturally regarded our regulated life as self-imposed torture. "Those people work on a treadmill", said the neighbors pointing in our direction. "Why, they go on a schedule, like a train or a bus."

So we did, but we kept a schedule because we had definite goals toward which we were working and which we planned to reach. No job is overwhelming if you have a general idea of what you are about, break the project into manageable units, put through these units one at a time and have the thrill of fitting them into the over-all pattern.

"Would I a house for happiness erect, Nature alone should be the architect. She'd build it more convenient than great, And doubtless in the country choose her seat."

Horace, First Book, 20 B.C.

"There is some of the same fitness in a man's building his own house that there is in a bird's building its own nest. Who knows but if men constructed their dwelling, with their own hands, and provided food for themselves and families simply and honestly enough, the poetic faculty would be universally developed, as birds universally sing when they are so engaged? But alas! we do like cowbirds and cuckoos, which lay their eggs in nests which other birds have built."

Henry Thoreau, Walden, 1854

"I count it a duty to make such use of the homely materials at hand, as shall insure durability and comfort, while the simplicity of detail will allow the owner to avail himself of his own labor and ingenuity in the construction."

D. G. Mitchell, My Farm of Edgewood, 1863

"One of the greatest pleasures of life is to build a house for one's self . . . I notice how eager all men are in building their houses, how they linger about them, or even about their proposed sites. When the cellar is being dug, they went to take a hand in it; the earth evidently looks a little different, a little more friendly and congenial than other earth. When the foundations walls are up and the first floor is rudely sketched by rough timbers, I see them walking pensively from one imaginary room to another, or sitting long and long, wrapped in sweet reverie, upon the naked joist."

John Burroughs, Signs and Seasons, 1914

"In the home-built house, life goes on enriched by a sense of beauty and an innate dignity that are left over from an older time, when hard work and infinite care, not money, were spent to beautify a house and its furnishings."

K. and D. N. S., Adobe Notes, 1930

"Nature, to my mind, gave men three materials, to serve him in the course of his life: earth, in which to grow food; wood, from which to fashion furniture; and stone, of which to build his home."

Frazier Peters, Houses of Stone, 1933

CHAPTER 3

WE BUILD A STONE HOUSE

Why stone?—Our rules for architecture—Selecting a house site—Pick and shovel work—Planning the forest farmhouse —The Flagg system—Building, setting and filling the forms Window and door frames—Changing the forms—Pointing and concrete finish—Fireplaces—Passion for stones—Roofs and roofing—Interior decoration—The whole building plan

WE BEGAN this book by describing our trek to Vermont and our buying first the Ellonen place and later the Hoard place. It was on the latter farm that we planned to build a home—a forest farmhouse.

The Hoard place had on it a half-dozen run-down but still usable buildings—a house and woodshed, a cow and hay barn with out-buildings, a horse stable, a pig pen and chicken-house. These buildings were designed to provide for the needs of a general Vermont farm, based upon animal husbandry. Since we had decided to keep no animals, most of the buildings were unsuited to our purposes, quite aside from their ramshackle appearance and condition. At the earliest possible moment, therefore, we gave the cow and hay barn, pig pen and chicken-house to John Korpi, who lacked these buildings and wanted them as much as we wanted to get rid of them. He and his son took them down and hauled away all of the usable material. The horse barn we kept as a temporary tool shed. The old house was used as a carpenter shop and storage space for lumber and cement during part of our building operations, before it too was torn down and given away.

We decided to replace these old Hoard structures with a group of functional buildings, all to be constructed of stone. We chose stone for several reasons. Stone buildings seem a natural outcropping of the earth. They blend into the landscape and are a part of it. We like the varied color and character of the stones, which are lying around unused on most New England farms. Stone houses are poised, dignified and solid—sturdy in appearance and in fact, standing as they do for generations. They are cheaper to maintain, needing no paint, little or no upkeep or repair. They will not burn. They are cooler in summer and warmer in winter. If, combined with all these advantages, we could build them economically, we were convinced that stone was the right material for our needs.

We are not trained architects and know next to nothing of the details of that profession. We have read on the subject, and have put up over a dozen buildings. In view of this experience, we take our courage in our hands, and state four general rules which we think should govern the architecture of domestic establishments.

Rule I: *Form and function should unite in the structure.* The symmetry and harmony of a building are not skin deep. They arise out of its innermost being. Neither utility nor beauty can be added to a building, as icing is added to a cake. The building should be so designed that it fulfills its economic purpose and does so without unnecessary expenditures of materials and labor.

Utility and beauty must be part and parcel of its line and form. As a rule, exterior decoration detracts from architectural beauty, although there are exceptions. Frank Lloyd Wright comments, "I have great faith that if the thing is rightly put together in true organic sense, with proportions actually right, the picturesque will take care of itself."[1]

Rule II: *Buildings should be adapted to their environment,* merging with it and becoming so indistinguishable a part of it that the observer must look twice before he decides where the environment ends and the building begins.[2] Both utility and beauty are qualities possessed by wholes rather than parts. If the environment permits of utility and is a thing of beauty, the building must continue the lines of that utility and fill out the exquisite balance and harmony which give rise to that beauty. "A building should appear to grow easily from its site and be shaped to harmonize with its surroundings if nature is manifest there, and if not, try to make it as quiet, substantial and organic as she would have been were the opportunity hers."[3]

Rule III: *Local materials are better adapted than any other to* create the illusion that the building was a part of the environment from its beginnings and has been growing up with the environment ever since. "The owner who sends far overland for unusual marbles or granites with which to build his house does not

[1] *On Architecture,* N.Y.: Duell, Sloan & Pearce 1941, p. 39

[2] "There is nothing obtrusive about old cottages. They do not dominate the landscape, but are content to be part of it, and to pass unnoticed unless one looks specially for their homely beauties. The modern house, on the other hand, makes a bid for your notice. It is built on high ground, commands a wide range of country, and is seen from far and wide. But the old cottage prefers to nestle snugly in shady valleys. The trees grow closely about it in an intimate, familiar way, and at a little distance only the wreath of curling smoke tells of its presence." Stewart Dick, *The Cottage Homes of England,* Lon.: Arnold 1909 p. 11

[3] Frank Lloyd Wright, *Ibid.,* p. 34

thereby achieve individuality, but the one who, for reasons of economy, digs up the forgotten local stone of the country—he does!"[4] "I was particularly anxious to demonstrate not only the possibility of employing the humblest materials at hand, but also of securing durability and picturesqueness in conjunction with a rigid economy."[5]

Rule IV: *The style of a domestic establishment should express the inmates and be an extension of themselves.* "A man's character emerges in the building and ordering of his house,"[6] says Richard Weaver. In a short story, "They", Rudyard Kipling writes, "I waited in a still nut-brown hall, pleasant with late flowers and peace. Men and women may sometimes, after great effort, achieve a creditable lie; but the house, which is their temple, cannot say anything save the truth of those who have lived in it."

With our four general rules in mind, we planned a long low building of native stone and local hand-hewn timbers. We would leave the natural ground levels and run the house along an uneven rocky ledge on the side of a hill. Three outside doors would have stone patios. A brown-stained balcony would front the house and look over Stratton Mountain. The roofs would be low-lying, broad eaved and stained moss green.

Snow conditions led New England farmers to locate their houses close to the public roads. The Hoard place buildings were farther back from the road than average, but they were on a low, wet flat, ill-adapted for housing purposes. Since good drainage is an essential feature of any structural operation, we were on the lookout for another building site.

[4] Edwin Bonta, *The Small-House Primer*, Little Brown 1925 p. 79
[5] D. G. Mitchell, *My Farm of Edgewood*, N.Y.: Scribners 1863 p. 84
[6] *Ideas Have Consequences*, Chicago: Univ. of Chicago Press 1948 p. 146

Skiing down the hillside above the Hoard place buildings, we ran through some brush and came onto what seemed like a low rock precipice. "It is as plumb as the wall of a house", we said. After the snow went off that spring we pushed our way back through the underbrush to view the rock. It was a split boulder, with an even face 26 feet from north-west to south-east, as vertical as though it had been set with a level, and, as it turned out later after we had cut down the trees in front of it and taken off some of the top soil, it was more than nine feet high. The back of the boulder was sunk in the hillside on the north-east. Its front faced Stratton Mountain to the south-west as accurately as though it had been set with a compass. (On a number of occasions, visitors who were not engineers asked us how we moved that great wall of rock into place.)

We had found our site. The split boulder would make the back wall of the new house. It became part of our living room and a faithful friend, whose twenty-foot-wide body kept out the north wind; who was cool to lean against in summer, and who brought a living part of nature into the home. From our second floor in back, the same rock formed a massive base for a stone patio which linked house and hill. The rock had answered the question of where to put our house.

We surveyed the surroundings. The thicket included some hemlock and white birch trees. We would leave them. Along the steep hillside above the site other boulders were scattered in wild profusion among the forest trees. The house would become a part of that setting.

The neighbors were horrified. "You don't mean to try and build up in that rock pile and brush heap!" they exclaimed. They called it "a bear garden", "a zoo", and, as the stone house went up, "a blacksmith shop". However, a comment from an 1863 volume fits our forest farmhouse. "I am gratified to perceive that the harshest observers of my poor cottage in the beginning, have now come to regard it with a kindly interest. It mates so fairly with the landscape,—it mates so fairly with its purpose; it is so resolutely unpretending, and carries such an air of permanence and durability, that it wins and has won upon the most arrant doubters."[7]

Our first building project was a lumber shed to house the boards and timbers for the building operations. Like all our buildings, it too was to be of stone. A decision to build a mere lumber shed of stone may seem too ambitious and formidable. Would not any old shelter do for lumber? Actually, the lumber-shed was an integral part of our whole plan. In Holland we had stayed in Eerde Castle, where two long low sheds fronted both sides of the roadway that swept up to the moat. We were building no castle, but the idea stayed with us. Eventually we had two long low buildings opposite each other (one, a garage and lumbershed, the other a guesthouse and toolshop) on the road that swept up to the main house. Building the lumber shed, the first of the stone buildings on the Hoard place, taught us many lessons.

Alex Crosby and his family were living for part of that summer as our guests in an unused schoolhouse which we rented from our neighbors, the Youngs. Alex was a newspaper man with a yen for creative manual work. "Isn't there some project you could assign me?" he asked, when they came up from Nyack. "Something I could do myself, at my own pace and in my own time?"

"Sure", we told him. "You might dig the foundations for the lumber shed."

[7] D. G. Mitchell, *My Farm of Edgewood*, N.Y.: Scribners 1863 p. 88

Alex went to work and made a fine job of it, under rather difficult conditions. For no sooner had he begun the digging than he ran on a shelving loose ledge which extended for many feet under one end of the building site. As we were planning to build with stone, we were forced to go down below the level where water would settle between the loose layers of this ledge, freeze to ice in the winter, heave and crack the walls.

As a matter of record, we did not get the foundation trench deep enough under one corner. Frost did heave the wall at that spot and gave us the one really bad wall crack in any of our stone-concrete buildings. This was not Alex' fault, however. During his digging, which lasted through several days, we all consulted over the knotty problems which broken ledges of loose rock always present to builders.

The lumber shed was 17 by 30 feet. That meant digging a trench 20 inches wide and about 90 feet along the four sides, getting out the dirt, removing loose rocks, of which there were many, and clearing off the exposed ledge so that foundation concrete would stick to it. We have helped dig many foundation trenches and seen many others dug in the rough terrain around that district. We have never seen a nicer looking job than Alex' trench when he had it ready for the concrete. He was justly proud of it.

While we are on this subject, we might note that many people use the phrase "pick and shovel work" with a curl of the lip. Make no mistake; digging to specifications is an art which few have mastered. Alex Crosby is one of the few we have met. Jack Lightfoot, one of our neighbors who helped us frequently and effectively with our building, is another.

The walls of the lumber shed were stone-faced outside, backed by concrete inside, built 10 inches thick. Door and window frames were made of hand-hewed spruce timbers, 6 × 6 inches, with plates of the same. Rafters were round spruce poles. Nailing strips, 1 × 6 inches, which went horizontally across the rafters, 16 inches apart, center to center, were the only milled materials in the building except for the lumber of which we built the doors. The windows, of course, we bought. To this building we later attached a 20 foot-long two-car garage, making the whole a synchronous 50 foot line.

We decided to construct the main house in three units,—a dwelling of livingroom, two bedrooms, bathroom, kitchen and cellar; a glassed-in passageway and pantry connecting to a large woodshed, half of which would consist of two rooms for sugar-packing and storage.

We wanted no complicated roof lines, so we designed two simple rectangular units with the long lines running from front to back. The passageway and pantry was a long, low narrow building joining the two main units. A second-story balcony and low overhanging eaves would give the structure an Alpine appearance. We planned to heat by fireplaces or stoves, with no radiators or central heating. We felt that steam heat, plumbing and electricity were not necessary for our comfort. Later, as electricity came into the valley we added electric light. Plumbing was to be taken care of by a running water toilet flushed with a pail, and a pump in the kitchen, which meant no pipes to freeze in winter. Our bathroom was to combine the Hindu and Finnish way of bathing. A slab of marble formed a bench against the parent rock, which became one wall of the bathroom. The floor we made with a central drain, and covered the concrete with a wooden grill. A chunk-stove heated the small room to 95° in a short time, and vessels of hot and cold water were used for washing and pouring and splashing. This built-in "Sauna" proved effective and enjoyable.

We wanted a farmhouse, not an imitation suburban or city home. We would build for utility and comfort and let convention shift for itself. We had, for instance, no front door. One entered directly into a roomy kitchen, low of ceiling, with exposed hand-hewn rafters, brown-stained panelling, wood stove and a pine plank table under broad windows facing the mountain. In the whole house there was to be no wall paper, plastering or paint. The walls were all to be wood panelled, the floors to be of stone. A colorful tapestry of books in rows of shelves, and the view through the windows, were to provide the decoration. Furniture of the simplest was to be home-made and built in wherever possible.

The first summer we contented ourselves with clearing away the brush, cutting the trees, and digging some foundation trenches. This sounds easy and simple. When we tackled it, we faced some formidable tasks. The trees, including apple and white ash, stood close together and were deep-rooted in the silt and rock-wash that had poured over the big boulder in successive freshets and floods.

There was an obvious location for the fireplace—in the east corner of the living room, right against the great rock. At that exact spot stood a sturdy white ash tree about 18 inches in diameter. White ash is proverbially well rooted. This one was no exception. We had to dig out the entire stump root by root. As the silt and loose rock offered us no satisfactory foundation for a fireplace and chimney, we went down seven feet before we reached hard-pan. Through the entire seven feet we chopped out ash roots. Along every foot of foundation trench we encountered stumps and roots, big and little. To make the work more exacting, the roots were woven and tangled through a never-ending maze of large and small ledge-chips and boulders.

The following spring we had to build a road to the new house site. In places the hill sloped steeply—as much as 15 to 20 percent. In going up this hill the truck wheels slid sidewise on the new grass, ground into the soft spring earth and then skidded on the resulting mud. We brought in stone and coarse gravel from the gravel pit and built up the road on the low side, load by load, until we got to the house site level. There we faced a new transportation problem. There was no spot large enough and level enough on which to turn the truck around. To meet this need we hauled up more stone and gravel and built a fill extending out away from the woodshed end of the house site. On its low side this fill was over six feet deep. Rock and earth from the foundation trenches and from the cellar helped us with this rather extensive project.

Like the foundation digging, the cellar looked easy. We proposed to put the cellar under the 11 by 22 foot kitchen, with its north-east end toward the big boulder. The ground was soft on top and we hoped that the silt and rock wash which lay along the boulder would extend far enough to make the cellar excavation a minor task. Alas, we had no sooner removed the top soil from the south-west end of the proposed cellar hole than we ran into a ledge of soft granite that went down to the cellar bottom. Fortunately the ledge was soft enough to be split off and removed with picks and bars. And by double good fortune these ledge slabs, exposed to the air, hardened up sufficiently to make acceptable wall-stone.

When we had cut the ledge down to cellar floor level we turned our attention to the other end of the cellar. We found no ledge there, and the washed-in dirt came out easily, but halfway back there was a good-sized boulder, five to six feet in diameter. We dug around it, decided that we could not lift it out of the cellar, voted against blasting it, inched it to the back of the cellar with bars, and walled it up, leaving a small but workable cellar about 12 feet square.

We found a spring in the back of the cellar-hole which might have made trouble for us. We concreted the sides and ran a pipe up to the kitchen sink. So we had an addition to the water supply which we piped down from a spring farther up the hill.

Having found running water, we faced the problem of getting rid of the overflow through a cellar drain. The land between the cellar and the hill slope was littered with boulders. With considerable difficulty we managed a ditch which missed the larger boulders and involved moving only the smaller ones. All went well until, about a foot above the cellar bottom we struck a hard granite ledge. One way out of the difficulty was to drill and blast—a matter of perhaps twenty feet. Instead, we filled up that ditch and dug another somewhat longer ditch which avoided the ledge and gave us sufficient grade for cellar drainage. Building operations, like true love, never run smoothly.

Our method of stone building was based largely upon the "Flagg system." Ernest Flagg was a New York architect who believed that people of limited means and experience could build permanent, beautiful dwellings out of native stone. They had done it in many parts of the world where stone was plentiful and Mr. Flagg felt that they should be able to do it in the United States. He therefore set about devising a method that would do away with the prohibitively expensive cut-stone, hand-laid masonry. His stone walls are concrete with field-stone facing,—the two being constructed simultaneously, as one unit. Instead of laying up masoned walls with trowel and level, he proposed to build a wall of sticky concrete, between two wooden forms, with stone facing to the front. The stone was to be not a veneer, but bonded into the concrete wall, with the rock often extending through three-quarters or more of the wall. Through years of practise Flagg successfully demonstrated that stone houses could be effectively and artistically constructed and at a reasonable cost.[8] "The Flagg methods enable the ordinary person, contractor, or clerk, to build a house of stone at a saving of one third the cost."[9]

Flagg laid down four basic propositions[10]:—(1) Stone buildings should be kept low, because after they reach a height of five feet, the cost of lifting the stone and concrete increase progressively with the height. If a second story is needed, it should be based on dormer construction. (2) Cellar space should be reduced to a minimum and all possible floor areas should be of concrete, laid on the earth. If it is desired, other types of flooring may be used over the concrete. Heating pipes and wires can be laid in conduits or channels. (3) The house should be a unit, with door and window frames of solid material, built into the stone and concrete walls, and without trim. (4) The walls are to be built in movable forms.

We would like to add three other points based on our experience in using aspects of this system. (5) Keep the roof lines as simple as possible,—few if any dormers or extra angles. (6)

---

[8] "Little accustomed as we are to stone buildings, it may be thought by many to erect such an one would be a great undertaking, yet it may be done without either great expense, nor much difficulty. Hammered or chiseled stone is adapted to public buildings, or the houses of the wealthy, and is expensive; but comfortable, decent houses may be built with common stone, such as we would use for good field walls. Such stones laid in strong mortar, will make an excellent building, either by facing the wall with stones, if fit for the purpose, or by rough casting the wall after it is built." J. M. Gourgas, in *New England Farmer*, 1/25/1828 p. 209

[9] Harold Cary, *Build a Home—Save a Third*, N.Y.: Reynolds 1924 p. 105

[10] *Small Houses*, N.Y.: Scribners 1921

Make all shapes as regular as possible, eliminating excrescences and cutting corners down to a minimum. (7) Build large enough, because stone walls once built are hard to break down if additions are desired.

Flagg's most important innovation was his fourth point— movable forms. Forms are scaffoldings built to hold concrete while it is setting. When the concrete has hardened, the forms are removed. Forms must be sturdy enough and braced enough to contain the fresh concrete without bulging or buckling. If they move from their assigned place, irregularities appear in the hardened concrete. Usually the forms are built by setting up a framework of dimension timbers, fastening boards on the side of the timbers next to the proposed concrete mass, pouring the concrete, and then removing the scaffolding. Form building is expensive because much of the lumber that goes into the ordinary form is used once, for a few days, and then discarded. Flagg decided to use movable forms. He erected studs around his projected building, bored holes in them at frequent intervals, put wooden pins in the holes, rested his forms on the wooden pins and fastened them to the studs. The studs were on the inside of the wall, consequently the concrete was poured around them so that they became part of the wall and were anchors for the furring strips needed for paneling or lathing. Flagg's forms were made of 2×6 or 2×8 inch timbers, cleated together side by side. It took two or three men to handle a 2×18 or 2×24 sixteen foot form, especially on a scaffolding.

We experimented with various types of forms and finally adopted one easy to make and light to handle. Its greatest advantage was the elimination of Flagg's expensive bored studs. Our improved form was exactly 18 inches wide, and made of three six inch boards. We tried making forms wider than 18 inches, but found that they were very heavy and unwieldy, and were so deep that it was difficult to place the bottom layer of stone with precision.

The boards for a six foot form were cut to length and assembled. (The problem of weight has been met in much construction work by using metal forms or forms built of plywood. We used ⅞ inch white pine or spruce wood. Pine is lighter, but expands more when it is wet. Spruce is tougher and expands less than pine.) At each end we nailed a 2×3×16¼ inch stud with the 2 inch side next the boards, and flush with the board ends. On the ends of the studs we nailed a piece ⅞×3×6 feet, thus making a shallow box, exactly 6 feet long, 18 inches wide, and 3 inches deep on the inside. We then put in two more studs, 2×3×16¼ inches, 24 inches from center to center and centered in the form, thus dividing our shallow box into three compartments. We finally brushed onto the form a generous coating of used engine oil, and it was ready to set up. In constructing these forms we used six penny common nails because it is sometimes necessary to take a form apart, and six penny nails can be pulled and re-driven with little or no damage to the form boards.

Our forms ranged in length from 15 inches to 14 feet. All were exactly 18 inches wide. In the longer forms the studs were placed every 24 inches, from center to center. The end studs of each form were bored, to pattern, with two ½ inch holes, 16 inches apart, centered both ways. Since all forms were bored with the same pattern, all holes were opposite one another when forms were assembled. We used ⅜ inch bolts, some 4 and some 5 inches long, washers and wing nuts to fasten the forms together. For corners, we left one end of a form "open." Instead of a 2×3 stud, we cut a ⅞ inch board, 4 inches wide and 18 inches long, nailed it in place, bored it with the usual pattern, fitted it over the form at the other side of the corner and bolted it in place. For this purpose, on the inside forms, we used flat head or carriage bolts. Otherwise we used square head or machine bolts. The latter are easier to tighten and loosen.

These forms were so light that one person could handle a 14 foot form, though they went up more quickly if two people worked on them. In planning buildings we aimed to place our window and door frames so that our inside forms fitted exactly between the frames. Sometimes, but rarely, we made special forms for particular places.

Having built a set of forms, we were ready to put them in place. The foundations of the building had been poured, and evened up without making them smooth. (We always left the top of the day's work rough or rocky to form a surer bond with the next day's work.) Within a day or two, while the foundations were still damp, we attached a set of strings to the nails in the batter-boards and began setting the forms.

If the building was a small one, say 12 × 16 feet or less, we set forms around all four sides. If it was larger, we selected a corner, set forms opposite to each other, with the smooth side facing toward the prospective wall. If possible, we set up at least two corners and connected them with forms, because two corners are self-bracing. To separate the two wall forms, we placed inside spacer sticks of hardwood, 1 × 1 inch, cut to the width of the wall, say 12 inches. Next we fastened the forms together top and bottom with light telephone wire which went through ¼ inch holes bored in the forms, around a 2 × 3 stud if one was close by, otherwise around a 1 × 2 × 16 inch piece set vertically across the outside of the form. We usually inserted tie-wires at the top and the bottom around each stud, which placed wires every two feet along the forms. These wires were then tightened by twisting them, inside the forms, with a 20 penny nail, until they were taut. If the twist comprises 3 or 4 wraps of wire on each side of the nail, the wire will not untwist when concrete is poured. If it is less than 3 or 4 wraps, it is better to leave the twisting-nail in place and let it remain in the concrete.

We now had an open double form, 18 inches high, 12 inches wide inside, bolted loosely together and extending around two corners of the foundation. The next job was to tighten the connecting bolts and level the forms. On an irregular foundation, this required staking and building up under the bottom of the leveled form. At the same time the form was plumbed.

If door or window frames were to go in at this level, allowance had to be made for the sills. If panelling, lath, plaster or wall board was to be used for inside finish, furring strips had to be placed in the forms at proper intervals. If there were door or window frames, we fastened furring strips to the sides of the frames.

When this operation was completed, we had a level, plumb, braced form, sufficiently tight underneath to hold sticky concrete. We were ready to fill the forms.

Let us assume that the building is to have a stone face outside and panelled walls inside. Furring strips are placed at necessary intervals in the forms, and held in position by 6 or 8 penny nails, driven in lightly from outside. Scrap nails, driven into the side of the furring strips, will hold them solidly in the set concrete. If the furring strips are set carefully, they can be cut to several feet in length. Once their bottoms are set in hard concrete, they provide an excellent anchor for the forms.

Over the surface of the foundation about two inches of "sticky" concrete should be spread,—slightly drier than brick mortar and yet moist enough to work into the spaces between stones without running over their outside faces and leaving cement stains.

The original Ellonen farmhouse.

"Our new place was a typical run-down farm."

Setting supports for pea vines.

The most formidable problem was not the soil but the climate.

Scott Nearing tending a vegetable garden.

Preparing natural compost.

Shoveling a path to the woodshed.

*Maple sap must be gathered
before it ferments.*

Boiling sap in the sugarhouse.

Driving through the sugarbush.

Building with stone.

The first completed cabin.

The authors.

"Usually there was a period of music Sunday mornings."

"The food we produced kept us in good health."

Irene Strauss

There was a constant stream of visitors.

The upper garden.

"We built a house of stone."

Forest Farm, Vermont.

Flagg favored a concrete composed of 10 shovels of gravel, 5 sand and 1 cement. For most of our foundation and wall work we have used 6 gravel, 3 sand and 1 cement. Either formula will give a slow-setting, solid wall, if the gravel and sand are free from clay or loam. Under either formula a wall can be put up that is surprisingly cheap and sufficiently hard to be permanent.

Into the two inches of sticky concrete on the foundation surface we put a line of wall stones, placing the flattest faces against the outside form and fitting them as closely together as possible, yet not quite touching. There should be room for some mortar between. The larger and thicker these stones are, the better. Limit of size is determined by the cross wires which hold the forms and the 10 inch form space left by the presence of a 2 inch furring strip. Occasionally we moved furring strips or cut wires to get in a particularly desirable and large rock. Behind these stones, sticky concrete is shoveled, then tamped solidly against the inside form, under and between the stones and around the furring strips. The tamped concrete should slope at 20 or 30 degrees upward from the placed stones, toward the back form. This sloping bank of concrete enables the builder to lay a stone with a good face against the outside form, snug it into place with a few light blows from trowel or stone hammer, and then push the surplus concrete all around the stone, with fingers or trowel. Once laid in sticky concrete, such a stone will not move unless the form gives.

If the wall stones faced against the outside form are 6 to 8 inches in thickness, very little concrete will be required to complete this filling operation. If they are thinner, leaving areas or pockets of concrete, push ugly stones into this concrete—being sure they do not touch the form or the wall stones. The larger the ugly stones the better, because they take the place of concrete and strengthen the wall.

In all mason work it is better to begin with the corners and work toward the open walls, because the corners are more limited as to size and shape of stones. It is easier to find a wall-stone which will fill the final gap than it is to find just the right corner stone for the end of a wall operation.

We now had a line of wall stones stretching between two corners and for a short distance around each corner, backed by an up-sloping bank of sticky concrete. We next pressed some reinforcing metal into the concrete bank around each corner. The reinforcing should extend at least three feet each way from the corner. It may be standard ¼ inch reinforcing rods; iron pipe or any other iron or steel scrap with a minimum length of 6 feet will do. We have used doubled barbed wire with good results. We like to put in corner reinforcings every four or five inches as the form is filled. As with the stones, the concrete around the reinforcing should be tamped carefully to prevent air pockets.

Our next move was to put in a second line of corner and wall stones, facing the forms and fitted as closely as possible into the first layer. One stone should not be laid directly on top of another, but should cross the intersection, thus binding together the under-lying stones. A little experimenting will show how to get the desired pattern. The corners should be especially well tied-in, with alternate stone overlapping on each tier. As these stones are placed, our trowels brought the sloping concrete around them and tamped them solidly. Additional concrete was shoveled along the inside form and the operation was repeated until the form was full.

Our practice was to place a layer of stone along the entire length of form, or at least 12 to 20 feet, fill up holes, due to irregularities in the stones with small chinkers faced against the outside form and tucked into the concrete. If the job was well done, there would be several fairly level places on top of this line of stone. If there was such a spot 22 inches long (the distance between studs and wires) we picked a stone 22 inches in one direction and perhaps 10 or 11 inches in the other, set it in place and braced it temporarily. We did this at every possible point, so that the big open spaces were filled by big stones. Then we filled the intervals with smaller stones. In this way big stones got into the wall and gave a less choppy appearance, the forms were filled quickly, concrete was saved and pointing minimized.

With a good selection of well-shaped stones, it was sometimes possible, between tie wires, to fill the entire 18 inches of the form with one or two stones. A little care resulted in attractive arrangements of the stone making up the outside wall, and it was always exciting when the forms first came off to see the varied patterns and colors. It was like the unveiling of an art work. We still recognize certain rocks as old friends and delight in many sections of our own buildings. We knew our houses from inside out and placed each rock with loving care.

Experience has convinced us that it is unwise to let stones stick up above the top of the filled form. As surely as we did, when the concrete set, we might find wall stones which extended beyond the outer wall-line. Before the next form could be placed, these protruding stones had to be broken off or removed, with a loss of labor-time and a weakening of the wall.

Filled forms were covered with empty cement bags, or some other protection against sun or rain, and left for 48 hours. In the meantime, if enough forms were available, we set them around the other two corners of the building, and proceeded as before. "Observe in working up the Walls," says a builder of 1712, "that no side of the house, nor any part of the Walls be wrought up three Feet above the other, before the next adjoining Wall be wrought up to it, that so they may be all join'd together and make a good Bond, or else what is done first will be dry, so that when they come to settle, one part being moist and the other dry, it will occasion it's settling more in one place than another, which causes cracks and settlings in the Wall, and much weakens the Buildings."[11] It is good practice to have all four walls of a structure go up at about the same rate, making it possible to check dimensions.

Regular door and window frames (unless they are metal) are made of 2×3 or 2×4 inch material, which in its turn, is covered by trim. In practice, the trim is beveled, beaded and otherwise varied and decorated, giving a fussy, over-dressed effect. Cutting and placing the trim is time-consuming. Flagg proposed that the frames be made of solid timber, be built into the structure and not trimmed at all.

We decided to use 7×7 inch local white pine for door and window frames. We had the timbers sawed ¼ inch over-size, stuck up in a lumberyard over winter and planed to size the following spring. When the planing was done we put them under cover in our new lumbershed.

All frames were made in our workshop, with halved-corner joints. They were bored at each corner with a pattern which put two holes, slanted at 45 degrees to the right angle, at each corner. Inch dowel pins were then driven into these holes: The frame was squared, braced and taken to its place in the building. One or two of the larger window frames were too heavy to handle in one piece. They were built in the shop, assembled, tested for square, taken apart and reassembled on the job.

We prepared for either a door or window frame by making a concrete sill of the desired dimension, beveled away from the

[11] J. Mortimer, The Whole Art of Husbandry, Lon.: Matlock 1712 p. 280

building at the outside to carry off water. We usually gave a sill 48 hours to harden. We then put a layer of mortar on the part of the sill designed for the frame, set the frame in place, leveled it, plumbed it and braced it solidly in position.

The position of the frame on the sill depended on thickness of wall and the type of inside finish. Our dwelling unit had 12 inch walls and was panelled inside in a way that placed the surface of the panelling 1⅝ inches from the inside face of the wall. The 7 inch frame was set on the sill so that it was recessed 7 inches from the outside face of the wall, and therefore extended 2 inches beyond the inside face of the wall. When the panelling was put in place, the inside face of the frame extended ⅜ of an inch beyond the face of the panelling, thus breaking the line of panelling at the frame and setting off the frame from the panelling. There was no other trim.

Following this method of construction, we soon discovered that after the building was finished, the different rate of expansion for concrete and wood pulled the two apart at times, leaving a small crack between the frame and the concrete wall. We remedied this in later construction by cutting a square groove all around the outside of the frame and inserting a small strip of wood which projected ¼ inch or a little more beyond the center of the frame into the concrete. Later we improved this method still more and cut a groove half an inch deep with a bench-saw and set a piece of galvanized metal ¾ of an inch wide into the groove. This took less time than inserting the wood strip and served the same purpose of bridging the crack between frame and concrete.

When the frame was in position, we drove a row of scrap spikes into the frame where it was to come into contact with the concrete, and poured the concrete against the frame. As the concrete hardened, the spikes were embedded in it, making the frame an inseparable part of the concrete and stone walls.

After some trial and error, we learned that the house plates should be bolted down into the walls. The technique was simple. As we reached the top of the last form, we placed half-inch machine bolts heads down in the concrete, with a good sized washer held in a vice and hammered until it tightened around the head of the bolt. The bolt was set in the concrete so that its top end would be even with the top of the plate. If the plate was a 6×6, the bolt would stand up 6 inches above the wall top. A ⅝ inch hole through the plate and a small notch, made with a chisel, would bring the nut snugly even with the plate-top. One such bolt for each 8 or 10 feet would insure against the plate shifting sideways when the rafters went on.

Frequently door or window frames came up to the plate. In that case we put an inch wooden dowel through the plate and 4 or 5 inches into a 6 inch frame timber, effectually anchoring the plate, since the frames were built securely into the stone-concrete walls.

After 48 hours, we went back to the filled forms, removed the cement bags and set another set of forms on top of the first, evening the faces and driving 8 penny nails through the 1×3 inch flanges. If the filled forms were properly levelled, the second layer of forms also would be level. It remained only to bolt, space and wire them, plumb them, brace them, and fill them in turn with stone and concrete. After another 48 hours, the wires were cut and the bolts removed from the lower level of forms. The forms were taken off, and put on top of the upper forms and filled in their turn. Thus, 18 inches at a time, the wall went up. It is rather like the children's game of hand over hand.

With three dozen forms, ranging in length from 15 inches to

14 feet, we built some eight or nine stone buildings at Forest Farms over a period of thirteen years. At the moment of writing they are being used by a neighbor for building a stone house. In addition we have used the same forms for garden retaining walls, concrete culverts, swimming pool and the like. Each time we finished a job we scraped the forms, made minor repairs, oiled them with used engine oil, and stored them in a dry level place. With minor breaks and a few patches they are almost as good as brand-new forms. The form-cost per foot of wall space constructed with their aid has been almost negligible.

Finishing the wall was a simple matter. When the forms were removed from the outside of the wall, we were confronted with a straight, plumb wall cut up by openings between the stones. Sometimes stones fitted badly or were irregular, leaving holes as big or bigger than a goose-egg. Our first job was to snip off all the extending wires. Then we went over the wall with a hammer, clearing off flakes of concrete which adhered to the wall-face. Next we went over the wall with a pail of small pebbles and stone-flakes, filling the larger holes to within a half-inch of the wall-face. Then, with a whitewash brush and pail of water, or with a hose if one was available, we wet the wall thoroughly. We were now ready for pointing.

Using a metal wheelbarrow, we mixed three shovels of well-sifted, sharp, clean sand, with somewhat less than a shovel of cement (3½ to 1 is a good pointing mixture) and very little water. The mortar for this purpose should be slightly stiffer than brick mortar. It may be mixed with lime to whiten it or with some pigment to color it. We merely used a light colored cement. On a large building, with much pointing to do, care should be taken to get cement from the same carload for the entire pointing job. At the very least the cement should be of the same brand; otherwise there may be splotchy or linear variations in the color of the pointing.

The pointing mortar is placed on a hawk (a piece of flat board or metal 8 or 10 inches square, with a short, round handle at right angles underneath). The hawk is held against the wall, slightly below the opening to be filled, and the mortar is pushed and packed with the back of the pointing trowel, a bit at a time, into the opening until the mortar is flush with the wall face. There are several ways to finish pointing. One can make stylized and formal lines. We pointed the simplest way,—even with or slightly above the wall-face, letting each stone tell its own story in its own form and color.

Pointing mixtures made with our formula set rapidly. On a clear, dry day, within three or four hours, the pointing would be hard enough to resist a light shower dashing against it. If there was any danger of rain immediately after the pointing was done, the area was covered, as wet mortar washes out easily, smearing and streaking the wall with cement stains. If this does happen, muriatic acid will wash off the stain.

Where much pointing is to be done, it will be well to have a standard pointing trowel, supplemented with one or two cheap small trowels from the five and ten cent store. With a pair of sturdy tin shears the blades of these cheap pointing trowels can be snipped down to ⅜ and ½ inch width. These narrow trowels come in handy for all pointing operations. Friends and visitors are invariably fascinated with the filling-in job, and love to stand with hawk in hand, pecking away at the wall with one of these trowels and dropping mortar all over the place.

We enjoy open fires, so we planned fireplaces for every room. Even in mild weather there is something indescribably attractive and satisfying about the flickering glow of a wood fire. The heat thrown off may be negligible, but the live coals vitalize the atmosphere and the leaping flames enliven the surroundings. In cold weather, open fires contribute the tangy perfume of burning wood as well as welcome warmth. Thoreau considered his fire a friend: "My house was not empty though I was gone. It was as if I had left a cheerful housekeeper behind."[12] A room without an open fire in winter is almost as desolate as a room without windows.

Building one's own fireplace is a satisfying and rewarding experience. We rarely let a year go by without putting one up in a house, of our own or some one else's. Our friends called it a recurring disease. Kipling would have understood our passion. He wrote in *Something of Myself*, "How can I turn from any fire on any man's hearth-stone? I know the wonder and desire that went to build my own."[13]

We lived in an area of rapid forest reproduction, where beech, yellow birch and hard maple were abundant. Wood was our only fuel, and fireplaces were our chief means of heating, just as they were of the original settler. We agree with the squire of Edgewood who said, "The days of wood fires are not utterly gone; and as long as I live, they never will be gone."[14]

Since an old-fashioned fireplace allows something like ninetenths of the heat to go up the chimney, we used manufactured metal forms in most of our fireplaces. These reflect and distribute the heat quite economically, drawing the air from floor level through the scientifically designed boiler-plate chambers, heating it and circulating it. With any one of the several types of fireplace forms on the market, the problem of design and engineering is

[12] *Walden*, Boston: Ticknor & Fields 1854 p. 272
[13] N.Y.: Doubleday 1937 p. 191
[14] D. G. Mitchell, *My Farm of Edgewood*, N.Y.: Scribner 1863 p. 8

eliminated. The builder simply encloses the metal form with stone or brick to the mantle level, and then constructs the chimney. Anyone following the directions cannot possibly go wrong. Also, for ten cents one can get a United States *Farmers Bulletin* giving careful directions for stone or brick fireplace building.

With two exceptions we used tile in our chimneys. They reduce fire hazard and decrease the amount of creosote which sticks to the inside of a flue. They also make it more difficult for mice and squirrels to get up and down. When a chimney becomes well-coated with creosote, mice and squirrels can travel it as easily as you travel a woodland path.

Our fireplaces and chimneys were built with stone, but rarely was the stone cut. Occasionally we knocked a projecting piece from a rock. In chimney construction, where good corners are essential, we did a bit of stone trimming. But in the course of our whole building program, during which we used many thousand stone, almost all of the rock were "wild stone, untamed by hammer or chisel."[15] In his account of building Edgewood Farm, Mr. Mitchell says "I insisted that no stone should be touched with a hammer; and that, so far as feasible, the mossy or weather sides of the stone should be exposed."[16]

The best-shaped stone we could find were put in the fireplace supply pile. Since they were the prize ones, there was always the temptation to pick them over when a particular size and shape of corner or wall-stone was wanted. Occasionally we yielded to the temptation, but usually one or another of us was a self-constituted guardian of the fireplace stone pile and uttered a cry of anguish whenever any builder approached the forbidden area.

Chimneys may be finished, on the inside like the inner walls,

[15] John Burrough, *Signs and Seasons*, N.Y.: Houghton Mifflin 1914 p. 256
[16] *My Farm of Edgewood*, N.Y.: Scribners 1863 p. 84

with panelling, wallboard or plaster. All of our fireplaces were built with stone chimneys, exposed from mantel to ceiling. We like the ruggedness of a stone chimney. Also, if a fire is kept day and night, as in winter, the stones warm up and help in heating the room.

Some of our fireplaces were built with mantels and some without. The mantel-less fireplace is a bit simpler and more austere. A mantel, especially a low one, adds cosiness but collects trinkets. Most of our mantels were stone. Two were of wood. One of these we hewed with axes out of a curly birch log, 12 inches in diameter. It was a chore, but an object of beauty when set up. Some of the spans between the fireplace pylons were held up by built-in arches. Most of them consisted of lintel stones, thin enough to allow room for the smoke flue and smoke chamber, but wide enough and heavy enough to support the weight of the chimney. In all cases we put a piece of metal reinforcing inside and under the arch or lintel to help carry the load. The lintel stone of the 42 inch wide living room fireplace in the main house was formerly the doorstep of a neighbor's barn. He insisted it was the best rock for the purpose for miles around, and it was, but it was part of his barn. At his own insistence and with his help, the rock was detached with bars, and still aromatic of the barnyard, was placed in our living room fireplace. Our neighbor, Jack Lightfoot, now has a proprietary interest in our fireplace and often comes over to toast his shins in front of a glowing fire and his rock. His eye still searches for other choice rocks and he often tells us of new finds.

Others have had this same passion for stones, and a farmer-author of the middle 1800's writes: "There were, scattered along the roadside, as along most country roadsides of New England, a great quantity of small, ill-shapen stones, drawn thither in past years from the fields, and serving only as the breeding ground for pestilent briars. These stones I determined to convert into a cottage."[17] John Burroughs rhapsodized: "It seems to me that I built into my house every one of those superb autumn days which I spent in the woods getting out stone. . . Every load that was sent home carried my heart and happiness with it. The jewels I had uncovered in the debris, or torn from the ledge in the morning, I saw in the jambs, or mounted high on the corners at night. Every day was filled with great events. The woods held unknown treasures. Those elder giants, frost and rain, had wrought industriously; now we would unearth from the leaf-mould an ugly customer, a stone with a ragged quartz face, or cavernous, and set with rock crystals like great teeth, or else suggesting a battered and worm-eaten skull of some old stone dog. . . Then we would unexpectedly strike upon several loads of beautiful blocks all in a nest; or we would assault the ledge in a new place with wedge and bar, and rattle down headers and stretchers that surpassed any before. I had to be constantly on the lookout for corner stone, for mine is a house of seven corners, and on the strength and dignity of the corners the beauty of the wall largely depends. . . I looked upon the ground with such desire that I saw what was beneath the moss and the leaves. . . With me it was a passionate pursuit; the enthusiasm of the chase venting itself with the bar and hammer, and the day was too short for me to tire of the sport."[18]

We have gone into so much detail on stone construction because we enjoy the solidity and massiveness of stone and we would like others to have a similar opportunity, both of work and enjoyment. We are convinced that anyone who will follow

[17] D. G. Mitchell, *My Farm of Edgewood*, N.Y. Scribners 1863 p. 84
[18] *Signs and Seasons*, N.Y.: Houghton Mifflin 1914 pp. 257-8

these instructions can put up a satisfactory stone building if he is willing and able to take the time. If he does build with stone, he will get a thrill from the day he discovers a blue-ribbon rock and places it in its proper pile, until he finds the right place in wall, floor, fireplace or chimney, and sees his rock set and solid years after, built into his house.

Before building we discussed the roof problem in detail. Stone buildings with non-combustible roofs are proverbially fireproof and are insurable at about half the rate of a frame house. For a time we favored slate roofing, which was produced within a short distance of us. There were difficulties, however. Slate was expensive to buy and to lay; it was heavy; and in winter, water and ice tended to back up under the slate ends, freeze and crack or break the slate, especially on a low-pitched roof such as we intended to build. Wooden shingles were out of the question with us because of the fire hazard. Asbestos shingles blew up and cracked in high winds and were generally not too permanent. Finally we settled on double-v crimp galvanized steel, to be painted moss-green. We have never regretted the decision. The metal was easy to lay, the fire hazard from sparks or chimney fires was nil, and the roofs, painted every three or four years, last indefinitely. Some of our metal roofs have been in place for twenty years; they show practically no signs of wear and the upkeep costs on them are negligible. Metal roofs protect buildings even when no lightning rods are used, especially if tin or iron pipes are connected with the roofs and run into the ground.

We wanted a low roof-pitch. "What constitutes the charm to the eye of the old-fashioned country barn but its immense roof,— a slope of gray shingle exposed to the weather like the side of a hill, and by its amplitude suggesting a bounty that warms the heart. Many of the old farmhouses, too, were modelled on the same generous scale, and at a distance little was visible but their great sloping roofs. They covered their inmates as a hen covereth her brood, and are touching pictures of the domestic spirit in its simpler forms."[19] The Swiss type of house snuggling lowly into the hill pleased us more than the steep-roofed Finnish and American houses. In our district in Vermont all the roofs were steep, because it was said the snow slid off quicker. However, we found that even in a heavy-snow area like ours, metal roofs cleared before any others (and, while we are on the subject, we might note that aluminum clears sooner than iron, but does not hold paint as well and dents more easily). By using a metal roof we were able to lower the roof-pitch and still get rid of the snow without shoveling. We also wanted generous eaves and gable-ends, in the Swiss manner. The low roof pitch helped in this design and yet let light reach the windows, which were placed just below the plates.

Simplicity and convenience were our standards in finishing and furnishing the house. We felt that without frills, trim, painted woodwork, wall paper, curtains, plaster, carved and over-stuffed furniture and bric-a-brac, we would have the basis for a Japanese simplicity that would be beautiful in itself. "The construction," said Claude Bragdon of a lovely room, "was the decoration: when the room was built it was decorated."[20]

First, as to the wall finishing, this was to be an integral part of the house, not a plaster or paper applied later. Into the concrete wall itself, as we were building it, we inserted vertical furring strips. When the roof was on and the house enclosed, we put horizontal strips on the vertical ones. On the horizontal strips went a layer of building paper and over this our pine,

[19] John Burroughs, *Signs and Seasons*, N.Y.: Houghton Mifflin 1914 p. 252
[20] *More Lives Than One*, N.Y.: Knopf 1938 p. 165

spruce or basswood panelling. Thus inside of the stone and concrete wall was an air space and a layer of building paper for insulation.

We stained our paneling a different shade in every room. The walls mellowed with time and formed a fine background for the tapestried color of our hundreds of books. "The natural color and grain of the wood give a richness and simplicity to an interior that no art can make up for. How the eye loves a genuine thing; how it delights in the nude beauty of the wood. A painted surface is a blank meaningless surface; but the texture and figure of the wood is full of expression."[21] "Bring out the nature of the materials," says Frank Lloyd Wright. "Let their nature intimately into your scheme. Strip the wood of varnish and let it alone; stain it. Reveal the nature of the wood, plaster, brick or stone in your designs; they are all by nature friendly and beautiful."[22]

All our floors but the kitchen floor (which was over the cellar) were laid on the ground and surfaced with smooth flat stone. The giant boulder backing the fireplace in the living room, and extending into the kitchen and bathroom, gave further substance and stability to the monastic simplicity.

When building, even though it was to be a small house, we aimed at spaciousness so that no room was tight and cluttered. The living room was 22 feet long, one wall lined with books, 14 feet of rock wall and the fireplace at one end, and 12 feet of windows at the other. The ceiling was 9 feet high and crossed with heavy handhewn timbers. No old furniture was dragged in, or carpets or curtains. As far as possible all furniture was built into the original design and was an integral part of the architecture. Frank Lloyd Wright says, "The ideal of 'organic sim-

[21] John Burroughs, *Signs and Seasons*, N.Y.: Houghton Mifflin 1914 p. 259
[22] *On Architecture*, N.Y.: Duel, Sloan & Pearce 1941 p. 34

plicity' naturally abolished all fixtures, rejected the old furniture, all carpets and most hangings, declaring them to be irrelevant or superficial decoration.[23]. . . Swift sure lines and clean planes in every way make a better background for living than lace curtains, figured wall paper, machine carved furniture, and elaborate picture frames."[24]

Four summers of interesting, instructive and rewarding work were necessary before we were able to move into the new house unit. Each spring we made syrup and planted a garden. It was June before we could devote time to building. Four or five months later, heavy frosts ended concrete and stone work for the season. When we made our original construction plans we estimated that the building project would cover about ten years. It was eleven years before we completed our entire building program. We had not rushed. We worked at it when we could and were satisfied if we kept moving toward our goal.

During the time we were in Vermont we put up twelve major buildings and many minor constructions. None was of wood, one was entirely concrete, and two were metal sugarhouses. Five of the stone buildings were grouped functionally around the central dwelling house. We might outline here some of those which have not been mentioned previously.

Our first building was the lumber shed which we have already described. Later a 20 foot addition on the west end of the shed gave us a two car stone garage, with storage space for nails, chains, ropes, paints and some miscellaneous tools. The completed building provided a 50 foot stone windbreak on the north side of the truck garden, which extended 28 feet south from the wall.

[23] *Ibid.*, p. 187
[24] *Ibid.*, p. 211

When we got into our new house on the slope overlooking the Hoard place buildings, we gave the Hoard house and woodshed to Vernet Slason who was on the job with us. He hauled them home piecemeal and turned them into a garage-woodshed. We rebuilt the cellar under the Hoard house and readied it for vegetable and syrup storage. Above it we built a 12×12 foot room, which we used temporarily for a workshop. When we were able to do so, we built a 12×20 foot addition with a concrete floor north of the 12×12 workshop, connected the two buildings with a room and stone fireplace, furnished the old shop and connecting room with two double beds and a single one, built in a toilet and used these rooms as a guest house. The far room we equipped as a permanent workshop.

We put up an open-air 12×14 foot woodshed, with a stone and concrete wall on the north side and the other three sides open. Three concrete piers supported handhewn posts on the south side of the building. The woodshed was not expensive. The cash cost was $114.88. It sheltered an abundance of air-dried wood, which was essential to our economy, both for heating the house and cooking our maple sugar. In fact, so important is dry wood in a back-woods farm economy that a Vermont wife can sue, with valid cause for divorce, when her husband supplies her with green wood for cooking and heating.

We cleared off a partly exposed boulder 25 yards west of the dwelling unit, and on it built a 12×16 foot study, stone finished inside and out, with a stone fireplace and a 6×9 foot window overlooking Stratton Mountain. The cash outlay was $553.75.

Finally we pulled down the last of the Hoard place buildings, —the old horse barn, erected an 18×24 foot stone and concrete tool shed in its place, built a 6×18 foot sun-heated greenhouse against the south wall and put a small cabbage and celery storage cellar under the lower end of the building.

As the years went by we constructed a 9×12 foot cabin of concrete on an upper lot, adjacent to the sugar bush. It was just the size of a one-man tent. We put in a tiny fireplace, let guests occupy it in summer, and in winter used it as storage space for sap buckets. We also built a concrete culvert and concrete bridge between the garage and the road, and in front of the house poured a 12×20 foot concrete swimming pool, with permanent granite forming the bottom and the side toward the hill.

Our latest and last building venture in Vermont was a stone cabin in the woods, built for a friend, Richard Gregg, who had lived and worked with us long enough to know he wanted to settle in the valley. We supplied the land and the materials and half of the labor. He did the rest, and lovingly fashioned a house to his own taste and needs.

It goes without saying that we did not do all of this work by ourselves. A very few of our guests proved helpful. Jack Lightfoot, our nearest neighbor, born in London, England, his head brimful of witticisms, criticisms, suggestions and plans, worked with us off and on when he could take his time from his farm and other commitments. In his own words, he was "Jack of all trades, master of none," but an ever-present help in time of need and trouble. Charlie Sage and Adelbert Capen, both from nearby Bondville, two miles over the hill, helped us for several seasons. Both were our friends, handy with the axe and adze, but neither were extra skilled in the art of stone house building.

Vernet Slason, also of Bondville, did more work on the projects than any other person. When we began our building program he had just completed a long session in the hospital and was feeling poorly. He made part of his living at that time by filing

saws. We took some saws to him and he did a superior job on
them. A few months later we needed someone to help during
sugaring. Vernet agreed to try it. He turned out to be extremely
ingenious. He had carpentered, painted, fixed clocks and gasoline engines; he was good in the woods; he had sugared. With
his help we relaid the pipe system in the sugar bush and built
the new sugar house. He did stone work with us, carpenter
work, cabinet work, plumbing. For every problem he had a suggested solution, and he worked as fast as he worked well.

We should not close this chapter without a bow to our faithful
pick-up trucks, of many years and makes; to our indispensable
gravel pit, and the long lines of stone walls, picked from plow-
land and pasture by our predecessors. All of these were assets of
the greatest value in our building program.

Our experience leads us to believe with Flagg, that people of
moderate intelligence, little experience and slender means can
build with stone if they have the time, patience and the inclination. Once the stone building is in place, it becomes a thing
of beauty and lasts indefinitely. Stone construction takes time,
but tested by results, it is time well-spent. In any case, here is
one way in which a self-sufficient homestead can be established
and strengthened.

"I come now to discourse of the pleasures which accompany the labours of the husbandman, and with which I myself am delighted beyond expression. They are pleasures which meet with no obstruction even from old age, and seem to approach nearest to those of true wisdom."

Cicero, De Senectute, 45 B.C.

*"The prudent husbandman is found
In mutual duties, striving with his ground,
And half the year the care of that does take
That half the year grateful return does make.
Each fertile month does some new gifts present,
And with new work his industry content."*

Virgil, Georgics, Book II, 29 B.C.

"Doe you yet maruaile how I can delight my selfe with this so honest and profitable a quietnes, then which in the judgement of the holiest and wisest men, there is nothing more honest nor better, neither is there beside any trade of life more meet for a Gentleman, nor travaile more acceptable to God, then is the tilling of the ground."

Barnabe Googe, The Whole Art and Trade of Husbandry, 1614

"I consider the kitchen garden as of very considerable importance, as pot-herbs, sallads, and roots of various kinds, are useful in housekeeping. Having a plenty of them at hand, a family will not be so likely to run into the errour, which is too common in this country, of eating flesh in too great a proportion for health. Farmers, as well as others, should have kitchen-gardens: And they need not grudge the labour of tending them, which may be done at odd intervals of time, which may otherwise chance to be consumed in needless loitering."

Samuel Deane, The New England Farmer, 1790

"I have often thought that if heaven had given me choice of my position and calling, it should have been on a rich spot of earth, well watered, and near a good market for the productions of the garden. No occupation is so delightful to me as the culture of the earth, and no culture comparable to that of the garden. Such a variety of subjects, some one always coming to perfection, the failure of one thing repaired by the success of another, and instead of one harvest a continued one through the year. Under a total want of demand except for our family table, I am still devoted to the garden."

Thomas Jefferson, Letter to Charles E. Peale, 1811

"All men eat fruit that can get it; so that the choice is only, whether one will eat good or ill; and for all things produced in a garden, whether of salads or fruits, a poor man will eat better that has one of his own, than a rich man that has none."

J. C. Loudon, An Encyclopedia of Gardening, 1826

CHAPTER 4

OUR GOOD EARTH

Vermont climate—The pitch of the land and terraces—The
living soil—Making compost—Laying out a garden—Principles behind our gardening—Extending the garden year—
A pit greenhouse—Raspberries—Mulching—Sweetpeas

THE keystone of our economy was our food supply. As food costs
are the largest single item in the budget of low income families,
if we could raise most of our food instead of buying it on the
market, we could make a substantial reduction in our cash outlay
and in our required cash income. Was such a project feasible on
the thin leached soil of a high Vermont valley? Our concern for
home-grown food led to much thought, generous advice from
the neighbors and some experimentation, in the course of which
we decided to undertake a rather extensive garden project. This
decision brought us face to face with three stubborn facts, the
Vermont climate, the pitch of the land, and the depleted soil.

The most formidable problem with which we had to deal was
not the soil, but the climate. Someone has described the weather
in our part of Vermont as eleven months of winter and thirty
days of mighty cold weather. Experience showed that the author
of this saw was not too far from the truth. "The Spring visiteth

not these quarters so timely . . . Summer imparteth a verie temperate heat."[1]

We were located at an elevation of 1800 feet above sea level, in a valley surrounded by mountains, where the frost-free growing season was around 85 days per year. In 1947, bean, tomato and squash plants were damaged by frost in June, July and August, which meant frost every month in that year. We have seen our apple trees loaded with blossoms; then, on the 22nd of May, more than a foot of damp snow has fallen, crushing flowers and breaking down branches. This May snowfall was followed by a hard frost. Late in May we have seen the weather-vane shift into the north after a heavy rain, and in the course of a few hours have seen the thermometer drop 12 or 15 degrees and stay around 20° all night, taking fruit, blossoms, seedlings and even the young leaves of ash, birch, beech and chokecherry. We have had our last killing frost on June 5th, and on August 25th we have seen an entire field of potatoes, sturdy and green the previous day, frozen dead. A nearby fruit grower lost 196 out of 200 Baldwin apple trees during the cold winter of 1938. They were fine healthy trees about 35 years old. All these experiences spelled possible frost twelve months of the year. Could a vegetarian household survive in such a region? After twenty years of experimentation we can answer that question in the affirmative.

We knew our climatic limitations. If we were careful, there would be a chance for tender vegetables such as squash and tomatoes to grow and mature. Hardier crops like potatoes, beets and carrots surely would get by. Apple trees would survive most winters. Plum and pear trees might frequently freeze. Cherries and peaches were out of the picture. The trees that did survive would bear fruit perhaps two or three years out of five, because

[1] Richard Carew, *The Survey of Cornwall*, Lon.: Iaggard 1602 p. 5

late frost might catch the blossoms. Among the nut trees, only beechnuts and hazels could be counted on, and they bore crops about one year in three. Our food raising, if food raising we did, must be concentrated in a brief period of each year and even then we would be compelled to pick our varieties with care.

We were in Indian country, but in our neighborhood there were few arrowheads or stone axes. Why? The Indians had hunted and fished there, but they had lived in the lower valleys. Their camping sites were in Connecticut, not Vermont. It was too cold, even for Indians, up in those frost-ridden hills. However, we knew the old settlers had conquered the Vermont wilderness, endured the climate, raised large families and prospered. We decided that if farmers had survived in that valley for more than a hundred years, we might also have a try at it. But we had notice. We must watch our step or we might lose our shirts.

The neighbors saved us a deal of time and trouble with welcome advice. Arthur Young, in 1792, counseled the newcomer in farming to "look over his hedges, and see what his neighbors do with their land; let him walk about the country for the same purpose, and compare the practise which he *sees* with the opinions which he *hears*. It would be for his interest to be acquainted with one or two decent sensible farmers, that will not take a pleasure in misleading him; such are everywhere to be found."[2] We had such neighbor-friends. Jack Lightfoot had lived in the valley for thirty-five years. Floyd Hurd was born there, was part Indian and could smell a coming frost. They talked to us of their experiences. Then each spring as planting time approached they apprised and warned. In the autumn they watched for frost as a mountain climber watches for avalanches.

We put our kitchen garden on a level with the house, but,

[2] *Rural Economy*, Burlington, Vt.: Neale 1792 p. 102

thanks to our neighbors' suggestions, we also laid out a garden three hundred feet higher, on a shoulder of Pinnacle Mountain. (Cold air drains from the heights into the valleys. An early frost which wipes out valley vegetation may leave untouched locations only a few hundred feet higher, especially if there are no pockets to hold cold air and retard its normal flow into the valley.) We called this upper garden patch our "insurance garden." There we established an asparagus bed and a raspberry patch. It was there that we grew all of our corn, beans, squashes and turnips, our tomatoes, all of our cabbage family plants, and most of our eating peas and sweet peas. Taking one season with another, we estimate that the insurance garden was frost-free at least three weeks longer than the garden near the house.

Later, as our food needs grew with more people coming to Forest Farm, we started an intermediate garden on a piece of land that had been used by the Hoard family for potato growing. In this garden we grew strawberries, hybrid blueberries and potatoes—all of which thrive in acid soil. The berry and potato garden was open to the south, but protected by forest growths on the north, east and west. The soil of the area was an exceptionally fine sandy loam. The spot had a frost-free growing season slightly longer than that of the house garden.

Land in the narrow Vermont valleys slopes steeply. There are level spots in the valley bottoms, but these are generally swampy or else they are so water-logged in the spring that it takes weeks of good weather before they are dry enough to work.

Most Vermonters meet this problem by planting their gardens on the slopes. Every third year they break up a piece of sod land, cultivate it while the sod holds together enough to protect the soil against wash, and then sow the garden spot to grass or grain and break another piece of sod land. When we talked about terracing our gardens, the neighbors told us "You can't do that. Gardens here are good for about three years. You will no sooner get your terraces made than you will have to move the garden and start all over again."

We listened. But we had seen terraces in the Philippines, in Europe and Asia upon which men had gardened for hundreds and in some cases for thousands of years. If they could do it in China, Japan and Germany, why could we not do it in Vermont? While our neighbors continued to shift their gardens each time the sod rotted, we kept ours in the same place year after year. If land sloped more than two or three feet in a hundred, we put up terraces. We began by building them of loose stone. When we found that weeds and grass were hard to uproot from these loose stone walls, we turned to stone and concrete. Mulches and fall-sown rye helped to reduce top soil wash. We built up our gardens by hauling in any available top-soil and we increased its fertility by consistently making and using compost, which enriched the soil instead of exhausting it.

Soils in eastern United States have been cultivated for any time up to four hundred years. In Vermont the time range is about two hundred years. The farmers who had preceded us in the valley had broken the sod, cultivated crops during the growing season and left the unprotected soil to the mercy of sudden showers, driving rains, melting snows and high winds. Consequently, most of the top soil had been swept off the hills and a good deal of it flushed down the West River and the Connecticut into the sea. What remained of the top soil had been sadly depleted. Year after year the trace minerals had been exhausted, until the land was barely able to produce grasses and the sturdier forms of wild vegetation.

Anyone who hopes to make a good garden must remember

that vegetation draws most of its sustenance from top soil, which is alive. Healthy soil teems with organic life. Top soil is alive in several senses. It is alive because it contains large quantities of organic matter, made up of plant and animal residues,—leaves, twigs, grasses, manures, carcasses. It is alive with microscopic organisms which convert organic matter such as dead leaves and grasses into available plant food. It is alive with earthworms which work the land by passing particles through their bodies, extracting certain nutritive factors upon which they live, and casting forth the remainder to greatly enrich the land. Sir Albert Howard writes, "The casts of the earthworm are five times richer in available nitrogen, seven times richer in available phosphate, and eleven times richer in available potash, than the upper six inches of the soil. Some twenty-five tons of fresh wormcasts are produced every year on each acre of properly farmed land."[3] These castings are "neutral colloidal humus, the only form immediately available to plants."[4] Earthworms ventilate and drain the land as well as transform trash to balanced plant food. Top soil swarms with insect and rodent life. The richer the top soil in organic matter, the larger will be its living population (unless it is drugged or killed with chemical fertilizers, poisonous sprays or dusts) and the more friable for production and use.

Whole food can be grown only upon whole soil. If essential ingredients such as iodine and boron, for instance, are not present, the vegetation grown on the soil and the animals which feed on the vegetation will suffer from the same mineral and dietetic deficiencies.

Eastern people, the Chinese and the Koreans, for example, have been growing food on certain areas for thousands of years.

[3] Letter to the London Sunday Times, 2/27/1944
[4] F. H. Billington, Compost, Lon.: Faber 1942 p. 75

But they have been careful to put back into the soil everything that came from it,—vegetable, animal and human wastes. Western man has been following the opposite practice. He is dumping great quantities of city waste, including human waste, into the rivers or the sea, or else he is burning it. He is abandoning animal husbandry, farming with machinery, thus decreasing the supply of animal manure, harvesting crops and putting back on the land chemical fertilizers which contain little organic matter and only a portion of the elements removed from the soil by cropping. Open cultivation permits water and wind to move the top soil bodily and thus decrease fertility. Such practices erode and demineralize the land. On such depleted lands, whole foods cannot be produced.

Nature has been building soil for ages. It may be found on the floor of forests and in swamps, composed of decaying vegetation, plus the castings of earth worms, the droppings and, occasionally, the bodies of insects, birds and animals. In North American forests an inch of top soil may be built in from three hundred to a thousand years. Its essential ingredient is decomposing organic matter. The chief factor in decomposition is the teeming population of organisms which live in and partly compose the top soil.

Perhaps it would be well, at this point, to note an important fact about the soil of a forest floor. The forest is composed of many species of trees, shrubs and lesser vegetation whose nature is determined by climate, elevation, exposure and soil content. The composition of the forest floor is constantly altered by the demands of the vegetation occupying it. The hard maple requires a considerable amount of calcium. As the calcium is exhausted by the hard maples, the soil becomes less hospitable to maple and more attractive to some other species,—for example, spruce. Consequently, over the years, the hard maple will be replaced by spruce, and a hardwood forest will give way to evergreen. We have seen this transformation taking place again and again in areas devoted to the cultivation of the sugar maple.

Soil, such as one finds on a forest floor, varies in its mineral content and therefore in its capacity to supply the requirements of different types of vegetation. The forest floor mixture being a chance one, local conditions may provide it with an over-supply or an under-supply of essential minerals. Strictly speaking, therefore, to reproduce the conditions of a natural forest is not enough. Each type of vegetation requires soil of a particular mineral make-up.

Must we turn our depleted soils back into forest and wait thousands of years until they are restored to wholeness? Certainly not. We can build whole, living, balanced soil by composting. Compost is a mixture of topsoil and organic matter which has decomposed sufficiently to provide nourishment for vegetation. Man-made compost may be kept, from start to finish, under the control of the composter. Soil testing reveals deficiencies. Deficiencies may be supplied and the proper mineral balance of the soil may be re-established by putting into the compost the proper amounts of the necessary ingredients. Soils may be built and rebuilt with somewhat the same accuracy that metals may be alloyed. Largely, it is a matter of learning the facts and adopting appropriate procedures.

Agricultural experiment stations, located in the state agricultural colleges, will help by providing soil analyses which indicate the mineral ingredients present in soil specimens supplied by the prospective food grower. The analyses will show what minerals are present in sufficient quantity, and what are deficient or absent. With this factual background the compost maker can introduce into his compost the minerals that will restore the balance of a depleted soil.

In our early experiments with compost making, we used animal residues—chiefly manure. Later we changed our practices and made compost as it is made in the forest, with the products of vegetation. We supplemented this vegetation, much of which came from depleted soils, with ground limestone, ground phosphate rock, ground potash rock, marl, or colloidal earth. All of these natural earths contain a considerable variety of the score of trace minerals necessary to maintain the balance that will provide for growth, vitality and health in vegetable and animal life. As our soil was deficient in nitrogen, we also used cotton seed, linseed, soybean or alfalfa meal. The results far exceeded our fondest hopes and expectations. On gardens covering less than a third of an acre we grew enough food to provide everything except grain for half a dozen people.

Our compost making followed the general lines laid down by Albert Howard in his *Agricultural Testament*[5] and *The Soil and Health;*[6] by Ehrenfried Pfeiffer in *Bio-Dynamic Farming and Gardening*[7] and *Soil Fertility, Renewal and Preservation;*[8] by Eve Balfour in *The Living Soil;*[9] and by J. I. Rodale in *Pay Dirt*[10] and *The Organic Front.*[11] We modified their patterns somewhat to meet our particular needs.

We built our compost piles 8 by 8 feet square. For a small family we would suggest 5 by 5, or even 3 by 3 feet. The important point is that the piles should be small enough so that,

[5] N.Y.: Oxford University Press 1940
[6] N.Y.: Devin-Adair 1952
[7] N.Y.: Anthroposophic Press 1938
[8] Lon.: Faber 1949
[9] Lon.: Faber 1943
[10] N.Y.: Devin-Adair 1945
[11] Emmaus, Pa.: Rodale Press 1949

with the available organic matter, each pile can be completed in two or three weeks. Some English composters recommend 2 by 2 foot piles for very small families or single persons. As the volume of the pile grows smaller, its capacity to produce internal heat decreases. Internal heat is one of the essential factors in the destruction of weed seed and the elimination of fungus enemies and in the rapid break-down of organic matter.

For our compost making we picked a well-drained shady spot, dug away the sod, laid it to one side, then took out 6 to 8 inches of top soil and laid that in a separate pile. Into this excavation we put a foot of coarse organic matter—pea vines, corn stalks, hay, straw, weeds, cabbage stalks. If materials destined for compost are wilted by lying at least a day in the sun, so much the better. Fresh cut vegetation, put immediately into a compost pile, is likely to go sour and retard the process of disintegration.

Materials used for compost are likely to be sleazy and messy, and so broken up that they do not pile neatly. Therefore a bin or crib is advantageous if not necessary. After some experimenting we built a type of open log cabin container, of poles 2 to 3 inches in diameter, cut from such inferior wood as poplar, white birch, hemlock or cherry. During our woodcutting season we made a point of converting all suitable straight material into compost poles, and storing them near our compost areas. We began to build our compost bin by laying four 8 foot poles around the sides of the square hole, with the ends of the poles lapping at the corners. As we added material to the pile, more poles were laid up, criss cross, around the pile. We continued this building process until the pile was approximately 5 feet high.

On the first layer of compost material (that is, at about ground level) we set up a ventilating system, consisting of three or four small poles, 8 feet long, bunched together horizontally across the center of the pile, with ends resting on the side poles. With a bar we made holes at two points along these ventilator poles (dividing the distance into three equal sections) and put in two vertical bundles each, containing three or four light poles 5 or 6 feet long. These we fastened together with wire. As the pile grew, air circulated along the horizontal bundle of poles and up through the vertical bundles. Compost piles smaller than 6 × 6 feet require only one vertical ventilator, placed at the center of the horizontal vent poles.

Compost piles are built with the materials at hand. These vary with the locality and the season. In Vermont, near each composting area, we kept a stack of straw or hay, a crib of autumn leaves, a bin of sawdust, a pile of sods and one of topsoil. These materials could usually be had for the hauling. Whenever they became available we picked them up and put them in their respective bins. Hay and autumn leaves were abundant only once each year, when we aimed to store enough to last until the following season.

Each day brought garbage from the house, weeds and tops from the garden, grass cuttings and trash from the flowerbeds. We used every available bit of organic matter,—never paper. These materials went on the current compost pile until they filled about 4 to 6 inches in depth. Since the organisms which break down the organic matter live in top soil, we sprinkled a thin layer of topsoil (half an inch to an inch) on this organic matter. Next we added a sprinkling of ground phosphate rock, followed by a thin layer of forest leaves from the storage pile kept for the purpose, with another sprinkling of top soil, and a light dressing of ground potash sand. Then came a layer of hay or straw, followed by a light dressing of sawdust, a sprinkling of topsoil and of cottonseed or other meal. Next, we applied a thin layer of sod, broken up and turned upside down with a scattering of lime-stone. That was our sequence. When it was completed we did the same things over again until the pile was breast or chin high. As the pile went up we edged it with the 8 foot compost poles. We topped off the pile with inverted sods and a thick covering of hay or straw to discourage weed growth, retain moisture and shut out direct sunlight.

It is better to build a compost pile a bit at a time, over a period of at least ten days to two weeks. If built in a day or two, it sinks too much. The pile should be damp, but not wet. In a dry spell this means some watering. If it is properly built, within a few days of completion it will heat to around 150°, thus speeding the breakdown of organic matter and disposing of weed seeds by germinating them. Unless the pile heats, the weed seeds may survive and be returned to the garden.

When the pile has cooled a bit, earth worms and worm capsules can be inserted. If the pile is sufficiently moist, the worms will work their way through it, breaking down the organic matter as they go. If no earth worms are available, the pile can be turned by forking or shoveling the material into a new hole dug beside the old pile. Usually we also put into the finished pile a small quantity of herbal activator, which speeds decomposition.

Activators are designed to speed up bacterial action, to attract earth worms and to expedite the disintegration of organic matter. Usually a small quantity is dissolved in water which may be sprinkled on successive layers or poured into holes made by a crowbar from top to bottom of the finished compost pile. After making compost with and without activators, we believe that they speed up the process, but that, if one is in no hurry, equally good compost may be made without them.

If the pile is kept damp and the weather is warm, the compost will be available for use on the garden in from sixty to ninety days. In the course of that period the varied materials composing the pile will be reduced to a rich, sweet-smelling earthy mass closely resembling the black wood dirt picked up on a forest floor. The pile will be more completely broken down if a longer time is allowed. Some organic gardeners recommend leaving compost for as long as three years.

Good compost can be made, as it is on the forest floor, without introducing anything foreign in the way of phosphate rock, potash, cottonseed meal or lime, activator or worms, and without turning the pile, but these elements help speed the breakdown of organic matter. On a piece of depleted demineralized soil, such as ours was, the addition of specific absent or deficient minerals stepped up the restoration of soil balance.

For years we put nothing on our garden except compost. We fed the soil live food, not dead, inert, synthetic or artificial fertilizers. The resulting garden produce was superb in quality, abundant, and of splendid color and flavor. And year by year we added to the volume of top soil as well as to its friability and productivity.

We laid out our garden so that the rows ran north and south, thus allowing the greatest amount of sun to reach the soil between plants. Each row was marked by a numbered stake. In our earlier gardening experiments the stakes were made of sawed lumber and the tops were painted before numbering. Later we used straight 16 inch sections of hard maple or ash saplings, an inch or a little more in diameter, pointed on one end with an axe and having on the opposite end of the stake, a small blaze, made with an axe, on which the number could be written with a lumber pencil. If possible the stakes were given a year to dry before they went into the garden. When gardening was over in the autumn, stakes were pulled, the dirt was shaken off and they were stored, dry, for the winter. Thus treated, they would last for several years. Tomato stakes and bean poles were made from straight saplings and were similarly cared for.

Above each garden we had a storage tank, from which we ran water in pipes to the garden and distributed it in the garden by means of hoses, laid to irrigation ditches between the rows. We did not irrigate regularly—only when the gardens got too dry, between rains. Some seasons we scarcely irrigated at all, but we had the water there if we needed it. In transplanting, the water was invaluable.

For the planning of the garden we employed several simple techniques that kept plans and garden and work in order. We had a loose-leaf notebook labeled "Garden Book" in which we put all information and material dealing with gardening. One section of the book was devoted to garden plans, including a free-hand map of the garden for two years, with proper crop successions and rotations, and a detailed plan, section by section, bed by bed and row by row. Entries in the garden book, under corresponding numbers, showed dates of planting, variety and origin of seeds, methods of treatment and results. We numbered our compost piles too and kept a record of each pile in a section of the garden book. These general records enabled us to test the efficacy of various gardening techniques and the reliability of different seed houses and nurseries. They also distinguished compost made with lime, which was not good for potatoes and berries. Year by year these records were made and filed away in the back of the book. By turning to them we could refresh our memories when we came to plan for succeeding gardens.

In late winter or early spring we planned our garden and ordered our seeds. Frequent changes in plan were necessitated by weather vagaries, and other unexpected events. But at all times we had at our elbows a pattern on paper which we tried to develop in the garden. Such a procedure of "think first, then act" helps to make gardening less haphazard, more interesting, satisfying and effective.

We come now to the principles which governed our gardening. (1) We wanted to live twelve months in the year from a garden which enjoyed barely three months of frost-free weather. (2) We wanted to eat fresh, unprocessed food. (3) We wanted a variety of garden products which would furnish a rounded diet. (4) We wanted to reduce canning and preserving to a minimum. Through the years we have been able to reach all four objectives.

Most difficult among these four assignments was the twelve months of fresh food from the garden. We approached the problem in two ways. The first of these two was eating with the seasons. There is something extravagant and irresponsible about eating strawberries and green peas in a cold climate, every month in the year. Such practices ignore the meaningful cycle of the seasons. Those who dodge it or slight it are like children who skip a grade in school, pass over its drill and discipline, and ever after have the feeling that they have missed something.

We seldom bought anything out of season, such as asparagus, strawberries or corn. Instead, we enjoyed thoroughly each food as it came from the garden. We began early in the spring with parsnips, the first thing available in our garden. As soon as the snow went, we dug them and had them for one meal a day for about three or four weeks. During that period they provided much of our starch and sugar. With parsnips went salsify, celery and parsley root, leeks and chicory. Then came six to eight weeks of asparagus, accompanied by dandelion, chives and multiplier onions. Before the asparagus was finished, we had begun on spinach, radishes, mustard greens, garden cress and early lettuce. Following that we had green peas, beets, standard lettuce, string beans and squash. In the height of the season came corn, tomatoes, shellbeans, broccoli, cauliflower and celery. As autumn approached, we turned to the cabbages, winter squash, turnips, rutabagas, carrots, escarolle, chinese cabbage, collards, with cos lettuce, fall radishes, spinach and beets, and, for the first time, potatoes and dried beans. We cultivated strawberries, raspberries and blueberries and ate them in season. These berries also grew wild in abundance, along with chokecherries, shad and blackberries. For other fruit we had pears, plums and apples.

After the snows, when the gardens were white and frozen, we turned to our vegetable cellars with their winter roots, cabbages, winter squash, potatoes, beets, carrots, turnips, onions, rutabagas, celery root, parsley root and pears and apples. The hardiest of these vegetables would still be fresh and edible up to the time the snow melted and we were digging parsnips once again.

Through this entire twelve month cycle, we ate a great variety of fresh food. It was garden fresh from the first thaw in February-March to the heavy snows of December. The balance of the time it came from an outside vegetable cellar. By following the seasons, we got a succession of foods—each at its peak. We enjoyed each in turn. We tired of none, but always looked forward to its coming in the new growing season.[12]

Gardens in our neighborhood frequently were made in May. By late August or early September they were neglected, weed-filled, insect-ridden and finished for the year. When frost hit us, usually in early September, our kitchen garden was filled to the

---

[12] Henry Thoreau wrote in his Journal "I love best to have each thing in its season only, and enjoy doing without it at all other times." Dec. 5, 1856

corners with frost-free plants. We are convinced that our early spring and late autumn gardens were more valuable than the summer garden.

Early spring gardens are made by wintering over leeks, chives, multiplier onions, dandelions, parsley, collards, chicory, removing the protecting brush and mulch when heavy frosts are ended and letting the sun bring them along. This gives one mature vegetables even before seed-planting time. Another help for the spring garden is a small, portable coldframe, made with a few boards and some window sash or cold frame sash, in which early radishes, lettuce, cress and mustard greens may be sown. Under favorable conditions radishes mature in three to four weeks. They are hardy and will stand some freezing.

Fall gardens grow out of summer gardens. About July 1st, as we removed radishes, lettuce, early beets and spinach from the garden, we scattered an inch of compost, worked it in and planted onion seed, beets, escarolle, endive, broccoli, chinese cabbage, kale, collards. A little later we planted oak leaf lettuce, cos lettuce, winter celery plants, spinach and finally mustard greens, garden cress and radishes. We did our last planting late in September or early in October.

When our cucumbers, squash, peppers and tomatoes froze, we replaced them with transplants of lettuce, escarolle, broccoli and kale, and with sowings of mustard, cress and radishes. On October first our garden was prolific, and greener than it was in August, because it was a greenness which is associated with autumn rains, night frosts and hot, humid and misty days. Insect pests had left for parts unknown. With the protection of a few evergreen boughs and some mulching with leaves, hay or straw, these green crops were available until they were covered by heavy snow. If the first snow was wet, frozen brussel sprouts, collards, escarolle, chinese cabbage, kale and parsley might be dug from under the snow blanket. At no other season are greens so delicious.

We further extended our growing season by a small sunheated greenhouse in which we wintered many plants and started others for spring planting. The south wall of our tool shed was 18 feet long—just enough to accommodate six cold frame sash, 3 × 6 feet. The tool shed, like all of our buildings, was made of stone. This gave us a south-facing stone wall against which we built a concrete and wood structure that held the six cold frame sash in a semi-horizontal position. On mild, sunny days in winter, with no stove or artificial heating, the temperature inside this sun-heated greenhouse went up to 100° unless we ventilated it.

We designed the place for raising celery, tomato, lettuce and other transplants for the garden. One October, however, we set out oak leaf lettuce plants, six inches apart. The lettuce had been sown outside early in September and transplanted to the pit greenhouse in mid-October; thus it had been hardened by early frosts. We continued to eat this lettuce until January 5th, and felt richly rewarded for our pains. We had almost bridged the winter gap in garden-fresh vegetables. We had not dreamed that lettuce would last so long in an unheated greenhouse under sub-zero weather conditions.

More surprises were coming, however. In the spring of the same year, following our success in carrying lettuce to January 5th, we discovered in the greenhouse, behind a flat, some of the lettuce plants that we had used for transplanting the previous October. They were hale and sturdy. Oh ho, we said, if these plants can survive the winter in a neglected corner, why not in the back bench of the greenhouse?

The next autumn we tried it. We cleared two inches of soil

from the back bench, replaced it by two inches of good compost, worked it lightly into the under-soil and set out eighty-eight heads of oak leaf lettuce plants from the garden. They were then about two inches high. As the plants grew, we scattered leaves among them to protect the roots against frost. We lost only two of the lettuce plants. The remainder we ate through the winter,—the last of them the following May. On two occasions that winter the thermometer touched 25° below zero.

The next winter we tried Simpson lettuce instead of oak leaf, with no leaves for mulch. Same result: lettuce until May. At the same time we included chives and parsley plants that had been growing all summer in the garden. These were equally successful. We had found an all-winter source of fresh greens. Had the greenhouse been roomy enough, we believe that we could have grown mustard greens, garden cress, leaf chicory and turnip greens all winter with equal success.

For a large part of the winter the top and sides of this unheated greenhouse were covered with snow. With the sun blocked from entering and the temperature down to 25° below zero we often found the lettuce frozen stiff. When cut under these conditions, it wilted immediately upon being brought into the house. Even plunging in cold water failed to revive it. However, if we left it uncut and waited for a warmer day or a bit of sun, the lettuce thawed out itself and stood in the greenhouse crisp and edible.

This discussion of gardening has been written mostly in terms of vegetables. Almost every word is equally applicable to flowers and fruit. To be sure, each flower, like each vegetable, has requirements which must be met if superior results are to be obtained, but the essentials of gardening are the same. Soil building practices result in fine quality vegetation, whether vegetables, fruits or flowers. Flowers and fruit respond to composting and mulching as do other types of plants.

We would like to report here on an experiment with red raspberries which turned out unusually well. We adopted the hill system. A stake two inches in diameter and eight feet long was set every six feet, in rows six feet apart. We put one or two Latham raspberry plants beside each pole. As these plants developed, we cut out the bearing canes in August or September, leaving six or seven new canes close around each stake. These canes we tied to the stake, waist high, with one piece of binder twine. In the spring, before the buds came out, we went over the canes, took out the weakest, reduced the number of canes to three or four, cut them to breast height, and tied them in two or three places to the pole.

Then we encountered the great problem faced by every grower of small fruit,—annual weeds and grass in the patch. If the weeds and grass are left long enough and if they get thick enough they choke out the berry plants. We decided to try a heavy mulch to choke out the weeds, and put about six inches of sawdust on the patch after the old canes were cleared out. The results were magical. Weeds virtually disappeared, except for milkweed, wild morning glory, sorrel and a few others that propagate from roots. Most annual weeds will not start in sawdust. The canes grew thick and high. Blights and pests to which red raspberries are subject did not bother us, though we neither sprayed nor dusted the plants. Fungus and insect damage were slight. Each autumn we added another six inches of sawdust to the patch. Such a mulch in the course of a year is reduced by packing, earthworms and weathering to about an inch in depth. The next year it is further amalgamated with the soil. After eighteen years of this treatment, with no fertilizers or manures, the raspberry patch was hale and hearty, all but weedless, in perfect condition, and had been raised two inches higher than the surrounding garden. The berries were abundant, extra large in size, beautifully colored and of excellent flavor.

We began our experiments with mulch in the raspberry patch. As the years went by we extended the principle to other crops with equal success.

Mulch is material placed on top of the soil in an effort to (1) retain moisture, (2) check weed growth, (3) keep the soil cool for certain crops, (4) prevent water and wind erosion, (5) attract earth worms at or near the surface of the soil, (6) provide additional humus and plant food as the mulch breaks down. Mulching materials range from stones and paper through hay, straw and other stalk growth to leaves, tree branches, wood chips, shavings and sawdust.

We regard the untouched forest floor as the most extensive and most successful experiment in mulching. There, year after year, leaves, branches, tree trunks, the droppings and bodies of living creatures are scattered over the earth's surface. Leaves and twigs from one year are consolidated with other refuse and soon provide nourishment for feeding roots. Year by year the underside of the forest mulch is converted into humus and incorporated into the forest soil.

After years of experience with the mulch in the garden, we are convinced that mulching practices are an indispensable supplement and complement to composting. In the course of our experimenting we have tried many mulching materials on different crops with varying success. Sawdust, especially that from hemlock logs, must be used with discrimination; we tried it on strawberries and potatoes with poor results. Plants like corn, beans and tomatoes prefer warm sunshine around their roots. Mulching these crops is a questionable practice, in our opinion. On the other hand, peas and potatoes, which thrive in cool soil, do phenomenally well under a mulch. For years we have grown our potatoes under heavy hay mulch from planting time to harvest, with no weeds, no hoeing, no bugs, no spraying and, at the end of the season, almost no digging, as the potatoes lie right under the mulch. In planting they are laid on top of the soil, covered with compost and mulch and re-mulched as often as the rains, winds and the voracious appetite of earth worms reduces the mulch layer to less than four or five inches.

One of our specialties in gardening was the growing of sweet peas. Each year we aimed to get in a double row at least fifty feet long. When we began in Vermont, we could not raise good sweet peas. The seeds germinated badly; when the seedlings appeared, they were destroyed by cutworms and stem borers. Plants that survived were sickly. Blossoms were short-stemmed, small, pale in color, and not too fragrant.

Once the soil was built up, the entire pattern changed. Young plants were sturdy; under favorable conditions they grew so high that the blossoms could be picked only from a stool or a step ladder. On a number of occasions they measured over eight feet from the surface of the ground. Flower stems were long. On many stems we had four to five blossoms, or even six. Flowers were large, fragrant, and of clear brilliant colors. We were able to repeat these successes year after year.

Our method of culture was simple. As early as the ground could be worked in the spring, we spread an inch or two of compost and worked it lightly into the soil. We made two trenches about three to four inches deep and eight inches apart, put in the sweet pea seed with a view to having the plants stand about four inches apart, filled the trenches with compost and firmed the earth by walking on it. As soon as the seedlings showed above ground we put a line of pea brush between the two rows and packed six or eight inches of hay or straw close up to the seedlings and across the intervening space to the next row. As the season wore on and the sweet peas grew taller, we renewed this mulch as often as necessary to maintain a depth of six or eight inches. Picking sweet peas involves much daily tramping back and forth with a corresponding consolidation of the mulch.

When the sweet pea vines were 24 to 30 inches high they began to bear flowers. Year after year they kept on bearing until heavy frost. Our flowers were better, in both size and color than those of neighboring professional growers. On one occasion we took a bushel basket full of sweet peas to an organic gardeners' conference which we were attending in early September. An expert, William Eyster, who spoke at the conference, was surprised and delighted that we had been able to grow such flowers and keep them going so late in the season. He said to us, "When you get back home, please send a bunch of those sweet peas to Mr David Burpee. His seed company built its reputation on sweet peas and at one time sold large quantities of their seed. Today this department is languishing because they say gardeners no longer have luck with sweet peas." We sent the flowers and received a friendly note of commendation and thanks.

Sweet peas grow while garden soils are well supplied with humus. Erosion, soil exhaustion and chemical fertilizers lower soil vitality to a point at which the production of good sweet peas is difficult or impossible. Composting and mulching, with the aid of earthworms, had brought our depleted soil back to a level of fertility which produced good flowers, as well as good fruits and vegetables.

Top soil like every other aspect of nature, can be plundered and depleted by wrong practices until it is all but sterile. Reverse these practices, build a living soil, and vegetation flourishes as it is reported to have done in the garden of Eden.

There is an old saying that we reap what we sow. Nowhere is this more evident than in the treatment of the good earth.

"Good dyet is a perfect way of curing:
And worthy much regard and health assuring.
A King that cannot rule him in his dyet,
Will hardly rule his Realme in peace and quiet."

Regimen Sanitatis Salernitanum, *11th century*

"Go, tell them what thou bringst exceeds the wealth
Of al these Countries, for thou bringst them health."

John Helme, The Englishman's Doctor, *1608*

"If you shall weigh with yourselfe your Estate and manner of living,
you will easily confesse with me and lay the blame upon your selfe for
such mischiefes. I do not direct my speech only to those who are already
affected with sicknes, but to them rather which yet inioy their good
and perfect health, to the end they may serve themselves with meanes
proper to maintaine the same. For how pretious and deare a treasure it is
to be of good health."

John Ghesel, The Rule of Health, *1631*

"Were it in my Power, I would recall the World, if not altogether to their
Pristine Diet, yet to a much more wholsome and temperate than is now
in Fashion."

John Evelyn, Acetaria, A Discourse of Sallets, *1699*

"Fly the rank city, shun its turbid air . . .
While yet you breathe, away; the rural wild
Invite; the mountains call you, and the vales;
The woods, the streams, and each ambrosial breeze
That fans the ever undulating sky—
A kindly sky! whose fostering power regales
Man, beast, and all the vegetable reign . . .
Here spread your gardens wide; and let the cool,
The moist relaxing vegetable store
Prevail in each repast."

John Armstrong, The Art of Preserving Health, *1838*

"I learned from my two year's experiment that it would cost incredibly
little trouble to obtain one's necessary food, even in this latitude; that
many a man may use as simple a diet as the animals, and yet retain
health and strength."

Henry Thoreau, Walden, *1854*

CHAPTER 5

EATING FOR HEALTH

What is health?—Nutrition—Whole food—Seeds—Processed food—Food profiteering—The milling industry—Food poisoning—Drugs—Malnutrition and physical degeneration —A personal and universal problem—Fresh foods all year— Winter storage of foods—Canning—Types of foods—Vegetarians and vegans—Our diet outlined—Meatless meals— Simplifying the feeding process

HEALTH is one of the most important elements in the good life. The better the health, the more adequate and satisfying the life. A design for living, a house-building program and an effective means of producing wholesome food are more or less meaningless unless they promote good health for the designers, builders and gardeners. It is one thing to produce quality foods on the land. It is quite another matter to incorporate these values into the human organism.

When we left the city and its environs to live in Vermont, we were in better than average health. Had we necessarily improved our chances for good health by moving from New York City to Pikes Falls, Vermont? Geographically, the answer must be in the negative. Vital statistics do not show any notable difference between the health of Vermonters and of New Yorkers. Personal observations in our valley and its neighborhood revealed numerous cases of digestive troubles, heart ailments, arthritis, cancer, goiter, tooth decay and mental deficiency. The people in Vermont were subject to about the same climatic conditions, ate much the same food and lived under many of the same pressures as the people in the city. If we wanted health in Vermont, or anywhere else, we would have to tackle the problem deliberately, as in all phases of the good life, and assemble the factors which produced it.

What is health? We have asked many doctors for a definition. The usual reply is "normal, balanced function" or "freedom from disease". When we asked what disease was, the answer came: "absence of health". So we were back where we started. The frankest answer we ever had came from an American doctor who had practised medicine for sixty years. To our question "Do you know what health is?" he answered without hesitation "Of course not". We believe we are correct in stating that no medical school in the United States offers a course on health.

The *Encyclopedia Britannica* has an article on the subject. We reproduce it in its entirety: "Health. A condition of physical soundness or well-being, in which an organism discharges its functions efficiently; also in a transferred sense a state of moral or intellectual well being". Thumbing through the *Britannica* volumes we have found lengthy articles dealing with scores of different diseases; health is given five lines. Medical journals and medical libraries abound in material on disease. It is rare to find in their pages any extensive treatment of health.

One such rarity is a book by an English medical doctor, *The Wheel of Health,* by G. T. Wrench. Instead of spending his time on the subject of sickness, Dr. Wrench asked, "What is health? Why are people well? Where can I find the healthiest people to study?" After much inquiry and research, Wrench concluded that the Hunzas, a tribe occupying a small valley in the border area between India and Tibet are the world's healthiest. Much of his book is devoted to an examination of the reasons for their state of well-being. He concluded that "Diseases only attack those whose outer circumstances, particularly food, are faulty . . . The prevention and banishment of disease are primarily matters of food; secondarily, of suitable conditions of environment. Antiseptics, medicaments, inoculations, and extirpating operations evade the real problem. Disease is the censor pointing out the humans, animals and plants who are imperfectly nourished."[1]

Wrench's wheel of health is a cycle from whole soil to whole, healthy vegetation, to the whole, healthy animals which consume the whole vegetation, and from the vegetation and animal back to the soil; where the cycle begins all over again, on a higher or lower level, depending upon whether the soil has been enriched or impoverished in the process.

"Health is wealth" is an old and a true saying. Health, wholth or wholeness is a primary and positive principle, which applies to human well-being as it does to other aspects of the universe. Health is attained and preserved by taking into the human organism solids and liquids (food and drink), air, light, sunshine and various more or less obscure sources of electro-magnetic, cosmic energy.

Human bodies are composed chiefly of water. Beside water they contain some twenty elements which are derived from the earth, mainly in the form of food. Ceaselessly the cells composing the human body are wearing themselves out through the functioning of tissues and organs, and the blood stream is busy carrying the waste products of body function to the lungs, the pores of the skin and other excretive agencies. Just as ceaselessly the food which enters the alimentary canal is being converted into

[1] London: C. W. Daniel 1938 p. 130

substances which can be used in rebuilding cells, tissues, organs.

Where food intake is low, in quantity or quality, the materials for repair and rebuilding the human organism are low in volume or in excellence. The nature of the materials carried by the blood stream to the cells, tissues and organs determines the character of the resulting bone, muscle and nerve structure. In that sense a man's body is composed of the materials entering it through the digestive tract and the blood stream, just as a building is composed of the materials reaching it over the railways and highways.

Normal bodily growth and function are dependent on the supply of nutrition through the blood stream. The nutritional elements which pass from the alimentary canal via the blood stream to the cells, tissues and organs supply the materials out of which the body is built and repaired. In this sense, we are what we eat. The human intake of solid and liquid food, water, air, sunshine and the other less tangible forms of matter and energy are the substances upon which human beings depend for their sustenance and their physical survival. Among these sustaining elements solid and liquid food occupy an important position. Each day vital organs like heart and lungs wear themselves out by their ceaseless action. In the course of a few years the more important parts of the body are broken down and the refuse is carried out of the body. Worn-out tissue is replaced by solid and liquid food, by air, by sunlight. Food plays a principal part in this process.

Each cell, tissue and organ has a mineral balance,—a workable relation between its component chemical elements. The balance varies in different cells and different body parts. Nutrition, supplied by the blood stream, must maintain that working mineral balance if the body is to be in good health.

Rebuilding in the body, as everywhere else, depends for its

success upon the quantity, variety and quality of materials supplied. A contractor needs stone, cement, lumber, glass and hardware in house construction. The body needs, among other things,
more than twenty minerals beside certain combinations of proteins, fats, carbohydrates and vitamins. The absence of a single
ingredient such as calcium, cobalt or vitamin A may throw the
organs of the entire body into painful disorder. Quantity and
quality alone are not enough; the food ingredients must be in
proper balance.

Each food contains a differing grouping of nutritional essentials. Only by combining the proper foods in a proper diet can
the health-balance be maintained. A food market displays dozens
or even hundreds of different foods. An uninformed shopper,
influenced either by whim, the colorful label, the radio or magazine ads or the bargain price, may upset the health of an entire
household by buying the wrong foods.

We noted, in the previous chapter, that most of the food consumed by human beings comes directly or indirectly from the
upper few inches of top soil. A whole soil is one that contains the
ingredients necessary to produce sturdy healthy vegetation of the
required variety and species. Different plants have different nutritional needs and offer various combinations of minerals, vitamins and enzymes to the animals and humans who consume
them. Soil wholeness may be upset by erosion, by cropping, by
improper fertilizers. Until the soil balance is restored, the products of an unbalanced soil will be unbalanced vegetation. If such
vegetation is consumed, it may transfer its unbalance to the user,
causing a person who eats "good food" by ordinary standards, to
be far from well.

Good food should be grown on whole soil, be eaten whole,

unprocessed, and garden fresh.[2] Even the best products of the best soils lose more or less of their nutritive value if they are processed. Any modification at all is likely to reduce the nutritive value of a whole food. Peeling potatoes, scraping carrots, milling wheat, cooking green peas, removes essential parts of the food, causes chemical changes, or drives off vitamins. Allowing foods to become stale or wilted has similar effects.

Whole foods are health-giving. They have another important virtue,—they are flavorsome. A whole raw apple or cherry, raw peas or corn, a whole raw carrot, beet, radish or turnip, a raw asparagus shoot, a leaf of lettuce, cress, spinach, endive, chicory, a ripe raspberry or tomato is more delectable to the unperverted taste than any product of the most elaborate food processing. We might remind our readers in passing that compost-grown fruits and vegetables taste better than the same products grown with commercial fertilizers or fresh animal manures. The latter have a sharp, strong, almost bitter taste in comparison with the bland, nutty flavor of the former.

A bean, pea, corn kernel or other seed, is a whole food. Each contains a life germ, a complete source of nutriment. All seeds, including grains, contain protein, oil, vitamins and the other potent life-giving sources designed by nature to nourish the germ until the new plant gets down roots and sends up shoots which will enable it to secure nourishment on its own behalf. Each type of seed is provided with a covering or skin, containing certain protective materials that will safeguard the germ until it gets

[2] "There is something in the freshness of food, especially vegetable food—some form of energy perhaps; it may be certain rays of light or electrical property—which gives to it a health-promoting influence. Certain it is that no synthetic diet that I have been able to devise has equalled in health-sustaining qualities one composed of the fresh foodstuffs as nature provides them." Sir Robert McCarrison, *Nutrition and National Health*, Lon.: Faber & Faber 1944 p. 11

a start on the life cycle. Each has a mineral balance adapted to
the peculiar needs of the plant into which it will develop. Sunflower seeds, for example, contain a calcium-fluorine ratio well-
adapted to preserve and maintain the calcium-fluorine content of
the human body. The people of East Europe, who are noted for
their good teeth, consume an enormous amount of sunflower and
squash seeds, cracking the shells with their teeth, and thus pre-
sumably getting some of the minerals contained in the shells as
well as in the kernels. Whole, entire, raw seeds, with the protein
of the germ, the fat in the oil, the starch in the kernel and the
minerals distributed through the protective covering, will provide a fairly rounded diet on which animal life can be sustained
for a long time.

There was a period in the history of human nutrition during
which men took food where they found it and consumed it on
the spot, as birds eat seeds, or insects and rabbits and deer eat
grasses and green-shoots and then move on. Under such conditions the animal living on vegetation secured whole food.

Western man seldom gets his food in its natural state. Such
food gathering is almost non-existent in a modern commercial or
industrial city where human beings seldom or never see their
food in its natural habitat, but get it, by way of the market, in
various stages of preparation, processing and aging. The classic
story of the children from the City and Country School illus-
trates this point. In order to contact the realities of life, this progressive school in downtown New York sent a group of children
on a nature study tour of the wholesale vegetable market around
Washington Market. When the students had sufficiently admired
the piles of bright beets, carrots, celery, cabbages, lettuce and
tomatoes displayed on the sidewalks and moving in and out on
trucks, the teacher asked, "And where do you think all these

lovely fruits and vegetables come from?" The answer came back, "From the A & P of course."

City dwellers suffer from a double liability: the foods which they eat are seldom garden fresh; in addition, most of them are processed. Go through any modern super-market; the majority of goods on the shelves are in cans or packages. Food processing, canning and distribution has become one of the largest industries in the United States. Modern markets are selling everything from baby food to dog and cat food in cans,—pre-cooked, mixed, prepared. Even people who have open land at their disposal find it easier to pick up these products in cans and packages than it is to raise them in a home garden. One lazy gesture with an automatic can opener; spoon the stuff into a pan; heat it, and the meal is ready. Thus an entire generation of humans is being raised, from infancy to maturity, chiefly on processed, prepared, canned and packaged factory foods. Most of such foods have been cooked, peeled, shelled, ground, sliced, minced, tenderized, pasteurized, or in some other manner deprived of their wholeness before they went into the cans or packages. The consumer does not have the entire food put before him, but only such portions as the food processers decide to include in the finished product.

The main factor in commerce which determines what parts of the food under consideration shall be eliminated and what portions shall be retained is profitableness. In order to make a profit, foods must have eye and taste appeal; otherwise there will be no mass sales. At the same time the product in question must have keeping qualities to reach the mass market and stay there in prime condition for an indefinite period. Not merely hours or days, but weeks and often months must elapse between the preparation of food and its consumption. Exceedingly high or low temperatures are necessary to preserve foods while they travel the tortuous road from producer to consumer. Any portion of the food which is specially perishable or might detract from its marketability is removed, even though it may be important from the health point of view. Marketability is the criterion, not the health of the consumer.

The milling of grain is a case in point. For a long time, humans stored their grains whole, as they came from the threshing floor. The grain, if dry, kept indefinitely, and because of the hard shell which covered each kernel, lost little of its nutritive value. Whole-meal flour, however, will not keep. Oxidation alters its chemical character. The oil in the kernel becomes rancid or evaporates. In a comparatively short time wholegrain flour becomes sour and mouldy. Therefore, under ideal conditions, when bread is to be baked, the whole grain should be ground. Dr. D. T. Quigley, in his book *The National Malnutrition,* says "The law in regard to milling and baking should provide that none but whole-grain flour be used and the whole-grain flour used in any bakery should be ground by suitable millers in that same bakery on the morning of the same day in which the baking takes place . . . For home use the fresh flour could be delivered daily as milk is distributed."[3]

When big business corporations moved into the milling industry they took steps to ensure the profitableness of their investments. Their first step was to find ways to cut costs,—in the apt words of the *Senate Report on Utilization of Farm Crops,* "to make a cheaper product resemble a better one".[4]

Two, they undertook to "refine" the flour, "to impart properties of softness and sales appeal",[5] to reduce it to smaller particles so that it could be swallowed with less chewing and would make

[3] Milwaukee, Wis.: Lee Foundation for Nutritional Research 1948 p. 90
[4] *Report 604 of the Committee on Agriculture and Forestry,* Wash. D.C., U.S. Gov. Printing Office 1951 p. 7
[5] *Ibid.,* p. 7

lighter breads and pastries. The germ and outer covering from the grain kernels were removed; with them went the oil, the protein and the minerals.

Three, they whitened flour, on the assumption that what is whiter is cleaner and otherwise superior. This had the added advantage of removing every vestige of livingness from the flour, which became inert and could no longer spoil. Flour was bleached by using one of the caustic chemicals such as chlorine, which sterilizes and reduces to a dead white color.

Four, modern milling involved processing in high speed metal machines which heated the flour and deprived it of any possible remaining nutritional elements.

Five, flours are now "enriched" by putting back substitutes, "synthetic chemicals",[6] for the essential ingredients removed in the course of processing. To quote again from the government report, "Many of the flours and breads contain phosphorus, flourine, silicon, alum, nicotinic acid, potassium bromate, and a score of other poisonous drugs . . . Bakery products, like so many of the processed foods, apparently offer those who would resort to chemicals and substitutes, a great opportunity for profit at the expense not only of the consumer financially but of the actual health of the consumer."[7]

Milling may sound like a horrible example of food processing. It is only one among many. We refer to it in some detail because the colorless, flavorless and lifeless white flour of the present day in the form of bread, crackers, noodles, cakes and pastries forms so large a part of the diet of western man. "Devitaminized wheat flour products imported into the city of New York constitute around 55 per cent of the whole food intake."[8]

[6] *Ibid.*, p. 7
[7] *Ibid.*, p. 11
[8] D. T. Quigley, *The National Malnutrition*, Milwaukee, Wis.: Lee Foundation for Nutritional Research 1948 p. 38

Among the vested interests who have come to the fore in the modern world there are those who deliberately devitalize, drug and poison the population for profit. Perhaps it may seem absurd, in this day and age, to write about deliberate poisoning. Most people associate the poisoning of food with family feuds in the Middle Ages, with primitive warfare or with an occasional bit of spite-work perpetrated in a fit of anger or jealousy. Research shows that the words are more applicable today than they were in the days of the Borgias.

Poison, says the dictionary, is "any substance which by reason of an inherent deleterious property tends to destroy life or impair health when taken into the system". Any food product which tends to destroy life or to impair health therefore may be listed as a poison. With this definition in mind let us refer briefly to bodies of fact concerning foods produced and sold in the United States.

1. Certain processed foods such as bleached white flour, white sugar and polished rice undermine health. White flour products lower intestinal health and harm lower nerve centers. White sugars impair teeth. Polished rice produces beri-beri and other deficiency disease. Pies, cakes, pastries, cookies, crackers, other products of white flour and of white sugar and white rice must be classed as poisons under the dictionary definition. Baking sodas, baking powders and common salt would come under the definition; so would irritating spices and sauces.

2. Food processors and packers in the United States are using several hundred chemicals to color, flavor and preserve foods. A study of the labels on the various food packages available in food markets will give a good idea of the prevalence of this practice. We walked recently through a supermarket and found a dozen products such as bread, pastries, oleomargarine, canned goods,

breakfast foods, puddings, cheeses, candies and carbonated beverages marked with the following chemical ingredients "to prevent spoilage": sodium diacetate, mycoban, benzoate of soda, di-sodium phosphate and citrates, cyclamate calcium, calcium chloride, polyoxyethylene and glyceryl monostearate, calcium propionate, acid phosphate, calcium sulphate, cyclamate calcium, niacinamide, sodium benzoate, pyrophosphate, carboxymethyl, sulphur dioxide, sorbitol, propylene glycol. Do we know what these formidable names are or will do to the product and to us? No. Do you? Probably not. Do the processors? Also probably not. They may be comparatively harmless or they may be extremely poisonous. "The inadequacy of existing laws to furnish safeguards is exemplified by the testimony of representatives of the United States Food and Drug Administration that, of 704 chemicals employed in food use today, only 428 are definitely known to be safe . . . The Federal Food, Drug and Cosmetic Act is not effective to prevent unsafe chemical additions to food before its sale to consumers. For it only applies to food after its introduction into interstate commerce; it may only reach the injury to a consumer thus sought to be avoided, after it has occurred; and it does not require an indicated advance scientific determination whether a chemical addition to food is safe, which alone can prevent that injury."[9] Apparently, in the case of at least 200 chemicals, no adequate study has been made of their effect on the human system. If they improve the looks of foods, increase flavor or postpone spoilage, they are used to the profit of the chemical manufacturer, the processor and the retailer. The eventual result on health and well-being is left as a concern of the customer. Well may the government report say "The increasing use of chemical

[9] House of Rep. *Report 2356, Investigation of the Use of Chemicals in Foods and Cosmetics,* Wash., D. C.: U.S. Gov. Printing Office 1952 p. 20

additives in the production, processing, preservation, and packaging of food has created a serious public-health problem".[10]

3. Foods are being poisoned in yet another way. Most fruits and many leafy vegetables such as lettuce, celery and members of the cabbage family are sprayed and dusted with arsenic, mercury, copper, sulphur and other materials intended to check fungus and insect pests. Even when taken in small quantities these materials poison the human system; in large quantities or over long periods they will cause sickness or death. Those of us who are increasingly aware of this danger cannot hope to wash away the poison with anything short of muriatic acid. These poisons are produced precisely for their lasting qualities. Read the advertisements of "the amazing residual effect of DDT"; "It Gets 'Em and Kills 'Em". "The new insecticides and fungicides are highly toxic, and they persist: that is why they are good."[11]

A government statement again warns us: "The public often feels that because something can be bought over the counter it must be safe".[12] "The housewife frequently fails to realize that insecticide such as DDT, chlordane, selenium, and many others in combinations, which can be bought over the counter, are deadly poison and must be used with extreme caution."[13] "Selenium is an elemental metal which in the form of selenium compounds is used as an insecticide . . . Animal experimentation has shown that three parts per million in the diet, as selenium, will produce cirrhosis of the liver and that, if feeding is continued, the animals may develop cancer of the liver. The residue remaining on fruits or vegetables sprayed with selenium compounds is rather high. For example, on an unwashed apple it

[10] Ibid., p. 25
[11] Eric Hodgins, Fortune, Nov. 1953
[12] Report 2356, p. 32
[13] Ibid., p. 31

may be as much as one part per million, and since it can penetrate the skin of the apple, it may accumulate in the apple in amounts up to three parts per million."[14]

"Phenyl mercury compounds are used quite extensively on fruit and vegetable crops as fungicides. Investigation of these compounds shows that they accumulate in the kidney and are very poisonous."[15] "Toxicity tests showed that a level of five parts per million (of DDT) in the diet of rats produced slight but definite liver injury. Later it was shown that cows sprayed with DDT, or fed silage sprayed with it, or even housed in a barn in which it was sprayed, would accumulate DDT in the fat and eventually secrete it in the milk. In a carefully controlled experiment, a dairy barn was sprayed in the same manner as would ordinarily be done by a dairy farmer. Nothing was sprayed on the cattle. Within 24 hours DDT showed up in the milk of the cows, reaching a maximum of two parts per million in about 48 hours."[16] "Chlordane is another of the chlorinated hydrocarbon insecticides which has been recommended and used in the household and on a large variety of fruit and vegetable crops . . . The Director of the Division of Pharmacology of the Food and Drug Administration testified that chlordane is four to five times more poisonous than DDT and that he would hesitate to eat food that had any chlordane residue on it whatsoever."[17]

An article in *The Scientific American* for August, 1953, mentions Hydrazine, which has a "toxic drug action". "Maleic Hydrazide is rapidly being adapted as a spray to stop the sprouting of onions and potatoes in storage; to retard the blossoming of fruit

[14] *Report 3254, Investigation of the Use of Chemicals in Food Production,* Wash., D. C.: U.S. Gov. Printing Office 1951 p. 4
[15] *Ibid.*
[16] *Ibid.,* pp. 3-4
[17] *Ibid.,* p. 4

trees until threat of frost is past." So now two of the most widely used winter vegetables may be contaminated with yet another poisonous drug.

4. Beside processed, chemicalized and poisoned foods, the food industry, through nationwide advertising campaigns, is selling a wide variety of consumable articles containing such habit-forming drugs as caffein, cola nut extract, nicotine and alcohol. All of these drugs are more or less deleterious or poisonous to the human system and bode ill for the health and well-being of future generations. In the United States alone more than ten billion dollars a year is being spent by the consuming public for products containing nicotine and alcohol.

Poisoned, processed and chemicalized foods result in malnutrition, since deficient foods, even when consumed in large quantities, upset the nutritional balance. Faulty nourishment has immediate effects, on body health, emotional stability and mental efficiency. Such effects extend all the way from a feeling of heaviness and drowsiness, through headaches, constipation and stomach aches to more acute conditions resulting from taking poisons into the system. This is one side of the picture and a serious side in view of the millions of American women and men who are constantly drugging and doping themselves instead of discovering the cause of the disorders.

Long-term effects of faulty nourishment which are far more important appear in the figures concerning sickness and death. A recent report of the Surgeon General estimated that 28 million United States adults are more or less handicapped by disease and its accompaniments. Of these diseased persons, a quarter were suffering from arthritis. The Public Health Service reports that in 1949 half of the deaths in the United States were due to heart disease and a seventh to cancer. Out of a total of 1,443,607 deaths, 720,497 were from diseases of the cardio-vascular system, 206,325 from malignant neoplasms, 49,774 from diseases of the circulatory system, 25,089 from diabetes. Contagious and infectious diseases were minor factors: influenza and pneumonia accounted for 44,640 deaths; tuberculosis for 39,100; poliomychitiz for 2,720; dysentery for 1,440 and typhoid for 161 deaths. In a word, people in the United States are suffering from breakdown of the vital tissues and organs. There is every reason to suppose that this breakdown is related to inadequacies in the food intake.

There is much debate concerning the connection between food processing and poisoning and the increase in the use of habit-forming drugs on one hand, and the extension of degenerative diseases over wider age groups on the other. It is only a few years since cancer was looked upon as a disease of old people. Today it is making inroads among infants.

Other evidence supports the assumption that faulty nutrition is causing physical breakdown. Pre-civilized peoples who have never used western processed, poisoned foods are free from the degenerative diseases which afflict western man. Wrench's study of "the healthiest people on earth", the Hunzas of the Kulu Valley, Kashmir, India, in his previously mentioned *Wheel of Health*, J. I. Rodale's *The Healthy Hunzas*[18] and W. A. Price's *Nutrition and Physical Degeneration*[19] show that when such peoples are fed western foods, they developed our diseases. Dr. D. T. Quigley, in *The National Malnutrition*, writes of the Indians of northwestern Canada who enjoyed good health and long life until they traded for the white man's food. They "took to this with as great enthusiasm as they did to alcohol; resulting in

[18] Emmaus, Pa.: Rodale Press 1948
[19] Los Angeles: American Academy of Applied Nutrition 1945

many cases of arthritis, tuberculosis, and tooth decay, with a shortened life period, and with lessened ability to work. The Indians in the back country who did not have access to the white man's food kept their good health; had no tuberculosis or any of the other diseases mentioned."[20]

Food processing, poisoning and drugging is undermining the health of the American people as well as yielding large profits to the individuals and corporations engaged in processing, poisoning and drugging. City dwellers, no matter how large their incomes and how much they can afford to pay for quantity and quality of foods, can escape the resulting dangers only by taking extreme precautions in regard to what and how they eat. Even country folk will fall a prey to this health menace unless they are able to raise their own food organically and reduce processing and poisoning to a minimum, or else find a means of securing fresh, whole foods, free from chemical poisons.

The reader may feel that we have taken liberties with his time and patience by this relatively long discussion of present-day nutrition in the United States and elsewhere in the West. We believe, as we have stated earlier in this chapter, that nutrition is one of the primary factors in determining the health, happiness and usefulness of every human being. We are equally convinced that the immense sums spent by the food processors, drug manufacturers and pharmaceutical houses for advertising, propaganda, lobbying and other types of "public relations" are having a deleterious effect on the well being of the American and other Western peoples. One of the chief factors that took us out of the city into the country was an awareness of the menace to health arising out of food processing and poisoning and a determination to safeguard ourselves against it.

[20] Milwaukee, Wis.: Lee Foundation for Nutritional Research 1948 p. 3

We admit that our solution of the problem,—raising our own food,—is a personal one since it leaves millions of people in the United States more or less helpless victims of the food industry. We should like to make two points in answer to this contention. The first is that each time even one individual or family wakes up to the situation and takes steps to ameliorate it, an advance is made if only a tiny one for the family or person in question, and for those they influence through precept or example. The second point is even more important. While it is true, at the moment, that all too few individuals and families in the United States are doing anything practical to meet the menace of processed, poisoned foods, we hold that at least half of them, if they so decided, could (1) produce part of their own food scientifically and organically on land that they own or could rent; (2) by creating an organized demand for whole organic food, greatly extend its production and availability; (3) purchase whole foods and prepare them at home instead of buying processed, packaged, chemicalized foods on the market.[21] In a word, our answer to faulty nutrition is not merely a personal one. In the coming growing

[21] J. I. Rodale in *"Prevention"*, a magazine devoted to the conservation of human health, has a further suggestion for those who are aware of the dangers lurking in the supermarkets: "If because of family pressure or some circumstance you cannot control, you must buy foods that have perhaps been treated with chemicals, dyes, preservatives or flavoring matter, write to the manufacturer or processor asking him whether such and such a product contains these substances. Tell him courteously but firmly that you do not wish to eat products that contain added chemicals, remind him that the Delaney bills are even now on the Congressional docket for discussion, and suggest that he be one progressive food processor who undertakes to remove chemicals from his products *before* the legislation is passed. Tell him quite simply that you would prefer bread that will mold, rather than bread to which a preservative has been added to keep it from molding. Tell him you prefer oranges with their natural color rather than oranges which have been dyed. Tell him that, regardless of flavor or color, you prefer to eat foods to which no artificial flavoring or coloring has been added." April, 1954, p. 119

season, if they were so minded, millions of United States families could begin to provide themselves with a considerable supply of whole, fresh, unpoisoned food and thus establish and preserve better health.

The food we produced organically during the regular May to October growing season kept us in good health. Then came the next question, how to make this fresh, delicious, health-giving food available throughout the year. Vermont winters froze our ground from November to April. If we wanted to eat our own organically grown products during that period we had to find a way to keep them. Our pattern for the simple life did not include icebox, refrigerator or freezing unit. We aimed to work out alternatives which would provide us with the foods we wanted, at the time we wanted them, and still leave us comparatively free of the power interests and merchandizers of large-scale gadgets. To winter our vegetables we tried vegetable pits or caches, dug in the ground and covered with branches, leaves and straw, with a breather-vent for circulation. In winters of steady cold, they worked well. In a winter of alternative freezing and thawing they were less successful. The vegetables tended to rot.

We finally decided upon root-cellar storage. In the course of our building, we made three cellars. The first one was under the kitchen of the main house. We dug it as we built the house, and designed it to hold maple syrup, preserves, juices and the fruits and vegetables in current use. It was never cold enough for permanent storage because it was separated from the kitchen by nothing more than a double wooden floor.

Our permanent vegetable storage unit was the cellar under the workshop, which later became the guesthouse. Fires were lighted in the room above this cellar only occasionally. The temperature there went to 20° Fahrenheit or lower during the frostiest nights of winter. The cellar had a spring which flowed from under a ledge. This running water helped to keep the temperature equable and the air moist. The floor we made of coarse gravel, allowing free flow of water and yet complete drainage. We equipped this cellar with shelves and storage bins, a foot deep and about three feet wide. Into these storage bins we dumped quantities of maple leaves, gathered when they first fell in the autumn before they became dry and dirty. Root vegetables and fruit were packed away in these leaves—first a generous layer of leaves, then a layer of vegetables, then more leaves and more vegetables until the bins were filled. On the top layer we put several inches of leaves.

The plan worked well. Whenever we wanted potatoes, carrots, beets, turnips, celery root or apples, we brushed away the top leaves and picked out the firm, crisp garden products. The leaves held off frost and at the same time kept the air from evaporating the juices from the vegetables and fruit. Almost every year we ate carrots, beets, onions, turnips, rutabagas, potatoes and apples from this cellar up to the July following the autumn in which they were stored. Many of these garden products lasted over into August.

Noah Webster, in *The Massachusetts Agricultural Repository* says, "I have fresh fruit, of my own raising, the whole year." For those who cannot get quantities of autumn leaves, he then gives his method of preserving for spring use. He recommends using layer upon layer of dry sand. "The singular advantages of this mode of treatment are these—1. The sand keeps the apples from the air. 2. The sand checks the evaporation or perspiration of the apples, thus preserving in them their full flavor—at the same time any moisture yielded by the apples (and some there will be) is absorbed by the sand—so that the apples are kept dry and all mustiness is prevented. My pippins in May and June, are as fresh as when first picked. Even the ends of the stems look as if just separated from the twigs. 3. The sand is equally a preservative from frost, rots, etc."[22]

Having found that our root cellar was too damp for cabbage, we built another type of storage cellar on higher land and with an earth floor, under the toolshed and back of the greenhouse. We strung a scaffolding of boards around the inside of this concrete cellar, drove in nails at intervals of a foot, pulled our cabbage up by the roots and hung them with strings, upside down, around the cellar walls,—no two cabbages touching. With that arrangement we managed to keep cabbage until the following May.

We also used this cellar for storing celery, celery root and parsley root,—pulling them on a wet September or October day before heavy frost, when plenty of earth would cling to the roots, placing four or five heads in an old sap bucket with a leaky bottom (for air circulation) and packed the buckets side by side on the earth floor of the cellar. Under fair conditions the celery would last for two months. If we took it from the garden just before the first heavy frost we had our own celery on the table at Christmas and New Year's. Curly endive, escarolle and chinese cabbage, similarly treated, kept fresh and good up to eight weeks. Witloof chicory roots we put in old sap buckets, covered them with earth and had chicory greens growing through the winter. With a little care, chives and parsley plants were kept growing until spring. Winter squash also kept in this cellar, though a dry, not too cool—not too warm attic is superior for the purpose.

By these various methods of storage we provided a year-round supply of fresh food. To be sure, during the depths of the Vermont winter it was not garden fresh, but, supplemented by greens

[22] 1804, p. 46

from our sunheated greenhouse, it gave us a satisfying and dependable supply of whole unprocessed foods. In most parts of the United States, weather conditions are less severe than they are in the Green Mountains, consequently such procedures could be made even more effective.

The reader, unaccustomed to such practices, may ask whether we did not tire of cabbage, potatoes, parsnips and the like "all winter long". We answer, no. We divided our garden produce into summer crops which we ate at once: peas, corn, lettuce and the like; summer crops which might be carried over winter by drying (peas and beans) or by canning (berries and tomatoes); and autumn crops such as cabbage, potatoes, turnips, squash. These autumn crops we almost never ate in summer. Take the case of cabbage. We never even planted summer or early cabbage. Our cabbage seed went in around the end of May or the beginning of June, in some row from which radishes or mustard greens had already been pulled. It was ripe for picking in late October or early November, when it was harvested and stored. We continued to eat cos lettuce, celery, collards, kale, brussels sprouts and broccoli, mustard greens, cress, escarolle and chinese cabbage (all of which are frost resistant) until heavy snows came in late November or early December. This gave us garden fresh greens almost to the end of the calendar year. Only then did we turn to cabbage, turnips, winter squash, potatoes and onions. Like everything else from the garden, we used them for an appropriate season, and it was so comparatively short that we never tired of our winter greens from the storage cellar.[23]

[23] "There is nothing which doth more agreeably concern the Senses, than in the depth of Winter to behold the Fruits so fair, and so good, yea better, than when you first did gather them . . . You will taste your fruit with infinite more gust and contentment, than in the Summer itself, when their great abundance, and variety, rather cloy you than become agreeable. For this

Another source of winter greens should be mentioned in passing, and a very important one, sprouted seeds. Asians have used sprouted mung beans successfully. Poultry growers sprout oats for their flocks. We sprouted mung beans, soy beans, peas and wheat successfully. The sprouts may be eaten in salads, thrown raw into soups, Chinese fashion, or prepared in any other desired way for the table.

We dried aromatic herbs from our garden,—basil, sage, thyme, summer savory, marjoram, parsley and celery leaves, all of which go well with winter salads and soups. Chamomile, peppermint, spearmint, raspberry and strawberry leaves we dried for tea. We hung the sprays in small bundles over our kitchen stove and when dead dry, crumbled the leaves and stored away in jars.

These methods of storage took care of the solider vegetables and fruits. What of the perishable foods? Was canning, that midsummer bogey of the housewife, completely done away with? Actually we did some canning, but a very little: fruit juices (raspberry, blackberry, strawberry, blueberry and grape), tomato juice, soup stock, and applesauce from our poorer apples (the "non-keepers"), to tide us over a possible "no apple" period in the late spring and early summer.

The fruit juice was put up so simply that it might be worthwhile describing the exceedingly easy and speedy process. The glass jars were sterilized on the stove. A kettle or two of boiling water was at hand. We poured an inch of boiling water into a jar on which the rubber had already been put, stirred in a cup of sugar until it had dissolved (we used brown or maple sugar, or hot maple syrup), poured in a cup and a half of fruit, filled the

reason therefore it is, that we essay to teach you the most expedite, and certain means how to conserve them all the Winter, even so long, as till the New shall incite you to quit the Old." John Evelyn, *The French Gardiner*, Lon.: Tooke 1675 pp. 263-4 jar to brimming with boiling water, screwed on the cap and that was all. No boiling and no processing. The raspberries, for example, retained their rich red color. When the jars were opened their flavor and fragrance were like the raw fruit in season. The grapejuice made thus was as delicious and tasty as that produced by the time-honored, laborious method of cooking, hanging in a jelly bag, draining, and boiling the juice before bottling. Our only losses in keeping these juices came from imperfect jars, caps or rubber. We found that two people could put up 15 quart jars in twenty minutes.

We made applesauce by an equally simple method,—the "open kettle" way. We had syrup boiling in several kettles on the stove (half maple syrup and half water). Into about an inch of rapidly boiling syrup we dropped sixths or eighths of washed, cored, unpeeled apples. We covered and cooked till a fork could pierce the pieces and they looked slightly glazed (the less cooking the better the flavor), packed solidly in sterilized jars, sealed and put away.

Our tomato juice and soup stock were made almost as easily. We filled two-thirds of a large 16 quart kettle with quarters of washed tomatoes. Then we cut and stirred in about a dozen fair-sized onions, a half-dozen bunches of celery (the green leaves as well as the stalks), a large bouquet of parsley, a handful of herbs (marjoram, basil, savory, sage or thyme) and a few peppers—all cut fine. No water was added. The mass was covered and cooked slowly till the celery was tender. Then the whole mass was worked through a coarse sieve. The juice we reheated to boiling, added a bit of sugar (maple), a touch of sea or vegetable salt, and the liquid was ready to bottle, with no further processing.

We made a soup stock with the remaining pulp in the sieve or collander. This was divided amongst several small kettles on the stove, with only sufficient water added to prevent scorching.

With constant stirring we brought the mass to a rolling boil, packed it into glass jars, and worked the contents down with a silver knife to eliminate air bubbles. To each half-full jar we added a tablespoon of salt, filled the sterilized jar brimfull, sealed it and put it away. This soup stock gave a zest and flavor to all our winter soups, and was more tasty than soups made daily during the winter from foods stored in the cellar. This was probably because the vegetables were picked and preserved at the top of their form and season.

"But to return again to Health and Long Life, and the Wholesomness of the Herby Diet"[24] . . . The foods we chose to live on were those that had the simplest, closest and most natural relationship to the soil. Jared Eliot called them "the clean productions of the Earth." All foods, animal as well as vegetable, come from the land, but raw fruits, nuts and vegetables are the simplest, come most directly and in the closest connection. They appeal to the taste with no adulterants, with no added flavoring or condiments, come crammed with vitamins and minerals and involve the least care and no cooking. We might call them primary foods.

Dairy products are foods at second or third-hand, reaching humans through the bodies of animals which feed on the produce of the soil. Milk is the secretion of the mammary glands of cows, goats or sheep. Cheese is a coagulation of the curd of this liquid. Eggs are the reproductive media of birds. Milk is a highly concentrated infant food, especially designed to stimulate rapid growth in the early stages of development. Human milk should normally be for baby humans, cow's milk for calves, etc. A calf doubles its weight in a month, a human baby in six months. Food intended by nature for one is not necessarily a desirable

[24] John Evelyn, *Acetaria*, Lon.: Tooke 1699 p. 127

food for the other. Adults of any breed should have been weaned and past the milk stage of feeding.

Humans eat another type of food which is the furthest removed from the soil,—the cooked carcasses of beasts, birds and fish. These animals have lived on vegetation or preyed on creatures which lived on vegetation. The human practice of eating the dead bodies of fellow creatures has gone on for so long a time that it is regarded generally as normal. In a recent study, *The Recovery of Culture*,[25] Henry Bailey Stevens attempts to show that this "blood culture", with which he also associates war, dates back in human history for only a very brief period. Before the blood culture, which began with the domestication of animals, there was a tree culture based on a diet of fruit, nuts, seeds, shoots and roots.[26] If this approach is factually correct, carnivorism is a recent phase in the history of the human diet.

Carnivorism involves (1) holding animals in bondage, (2) turning them into machines for breeding and milking, (3) slaughtering them for food, (4) preserving and processing their dead bodies for human consumption.

We were looking for a kindly, decent, clean and simple way of life. Long ago we decided to live in the vegetarian way, without killing or eating animals; and lately we have largely ceased to use dairy products and have allied ourselves with the vegans, who use and eat no animal products, butter, cheese, eggs or milk. This is all in line with our philosophy of the least harm to the least number and the greatest good to the greatest number of life forms.[27]

[25] N.Y.: Harpers 1949
[26] "Primitive humanity was, no doubt, like the anthropoids, mainly frugivorous." R. Briffault, *The Mothers*, Lon.: Allen & Unwin 1927 Vol. I p. 441
[27] "The use of Plants is all our Life long of that universal Importance and Concern, that we can neither live nor subsist in any Plenty with Decency, or

We aimed to keep our diet at fifty percent fruit, thirty-five percent vegetables, ten percent protein and starch, and five percent fat. The kind of fruits varied with the season. Its proportion of the total diet remained substantially the same. Of the vegetables we tried to have one-third green and leafy, one-third yellow and one-third juicy. This ensured us a rounded quota of essential nutritives. In the summer, fruits and succulent vegetables were at least three-quarters of our dietary,—in winter perhaps a third to a half. Our protein came from nuts, beans, olives and the proteins contained in vegetables and in cereal grains and seeds. We believe that a far smaller amount of protein is necessary and healthful than usually advocated. The craving for concentrated protein foods is an acquired and a dangerous habit, in that it over-energizes the human organism and overloads the system with acid-forming elements. Our fats were derived from vegetable oils,—olive, soy, corn, peanut or sunflower. We have a high opinion of the efficacy of olive oil. Avocado pears are also an important source of vegetable fat for people living on the vegetarian diet.

Our search for simplicity led us away from elaborate variety and in the direction of a mono-diet.[28] To eat little and of few

Conveniency or be said to live indeed at all without them: whatsoever Food is necessary to sustain us, whatsoever contributes to delight and refresh us, are supply'd and brought forth out of that plentiful and abundant store: and ah, how much more innocent, sweet and healthful is a Table cover'd with these, than with all the reeking Flesh of butcher'd and slaughter'd Animals! Certainly Man by Nature was never made to be a Carnivorous Creature; nor is he arm'd at all for Prey and Rapin, with gag'd and pointed Teeth and crooked Claws, sharpened to rend and tear: But with gentle Hands to gather Fruit and Vegetables, and with Teeth to chew and eat them." John Ray, *Historia Plantarum*, Lon.: Faithorne 1686 p. 46

[28] "It neither entices men to eat till they be unable for their affairs, nor brings it sickness; it affords strength, and prolongs life." Sir George Mackenzie, *A Moral Essay, preferring Solitude to Publick Employment*, Lon.: Sawbridge 1685 p. 123

things is a good guide for health and for simplicity. There are primitive peoples, for instance the island inhabitants of Tristan de Cunha, whose health and teeth are reportedly superb, who "never eat more than one kind of food at a time".[29] There are individuals in the West who do not mix vegetables with fruits, nor proteins and starches and acids, on the assumption that this facilitates digestion. These points need not be argued here. As a matter of fact, we are still experimenting on them ourselves. We do assert, however, that the closer one gets to a mono diet, the easier is the process not only of digestion, but of food preparation. Whole foods, raw foods and few of a kind make little work for the housewife.

Apply to vegetables and fruit the principles of wholeness, rawness, garden freshness, and one or few things at a meal, and you have the theory of our simple diet. In practice, the theory gave us a formulated regime: fruit for breakfast; soup and cereal for lunch; salad and vegetables for supper.

This fruit breakfast did not include the usual small glass of orange juice, a spoonful or two of berries or prunes or a dab of applesauce in a bowl with cornflakes or puffed wheat followed by toast and coffee. Our breakfast was fruit; fruit alone and plenty of it. It might be strawberry, raspberry, blackberry or blueberry season; we picked the berries in the woods or garden and ate them, perhaps half a quart to a person. Melons and peaches were eaten when in season. Bananas, raisins, oranges and dates were bought in the periods our local fruit gave out. Apples were the perennial staple as we had plenty of them on the place and they kept well all winter. Apples are a fine food, highly alkaline and extremely rich in iron and other important minerals. We often had a one-day exclusive apple diet to revivify and cleanse

[29] London *Times* 2/22/32

the system. Oranges we did not juice, but cut in sixths, longways, and ate like watermelons, down to the peel. Gourmets amongst us dipped whole bananas in honey and then in wheatgerm. Quarter sections of apples were dipped the same way, or spread with peanut butter. Nuts were often cracked and eaten with the apples. Berries were served with maple syrup or honey, or eaten dry. Breakfast was rounded out by a handful of sunflower seeds, herb tea sweetened with honey, or a tablespoon of blackstrap molasses in hot water.

Another fruit-derived breakfast item which deserves more than passing mention is rose-hip or rose-apple extract, which we often added to our molasses or our mint tea. Rose-hips are an important source of vitamin C, containing on the average thirty times as much as fresh orange juice. "Some species", says Adelle Davis, "have been found to contain 96 times the vitamin-C content of citrus juices."[30] Her cookbook gives methods (which we used) of drying and preserving the rose fruit. Our attention was first called to rose-hip juice when a neighbor, Lois Smith, prepared a supply one autumn and fed a tablespoon per day to Marshall and the youngsters. It cleared up their colds like magic.

People may feel that such a "light" breakfast would not stand by a working-man or woman till noon. That is largely a matter of habit. We have gone for months at a time with no breakfast at all and maintained health and suffered no discomfort though carrying on a full program of work. For ten years we have eaten fruit for our first meal of the day, and yet put in four solid hours at hard physical or mental work until lunch. We felt better, worked better and lived better on it than after a stuffy starch, protein-rich breakfast.

Lunch was ever the same and ever different: a soup and some

[30] *Let's Cook It Right,* N.Y.: Harcourt, Brace 1947 p. 488

sort of cereal. The soup was always vegetable but the ingredients varied from day to day, one vegetable usually predominating: potatoes, cabbage, carrots, tomatoes, onion, parsley, celery, beans, peas, beets or corn. We added dried herbs and sea salt for seasoning. Occasionally barley, soy bean meal, oats or rice were included. At this mealtime we ate all the cereal for the day: wheat seed, buckwheat or millet. These we bought in bulk (anywhere up to a hundred pound bag from local feed stores) and stored in tin ash cans. We soaked a few handfuls of seeds overnight, and the next day either baked them in the oven with occasional basting of water, or cooked them slowly on top of the stove in a double boiler. The grains swelled to double their original size and were delicious and nutty eaten either hot or cold, with oil or butter and vegetable salt, with home-made jam or syrup, or with a peanut-butter-honey emulsion. Two bowls of soup and all the whole grain one wanted was a man's meal and lasted well till suppertime.

Raised bread we never baked and seldom bought.[31] We got the same or better nourishment (and far cheaper) from the whole seed grain unprocessed. Occasionally we made corn-cob shaped "journey cakes" with coarsely-ground whole grains, corn meal, rolled wheat and oats, sweetened with maple syrup or molasses and moistened with soup stock and peanut butter or oil. After making carrot juice, the remaining pulp sometimes formed the

---

[31] "Bread on the whole is not a very satisfactory food, because it is very acid and on this account is apt to ferment 'and cause flatulence, especially when eaten with fruit; so in those inclined to flatulence the amount of bread in the day should be limited to small quantities. I have often seen flatulence disappear after cutting down bread and fluids. Bread is not only acid because of the acid salts of the wheat, but acid phosphate and calcium sulphate are often added in baking powders. This leads to retention and so bread is bad for rheumatism." K. G. Haig, *Health Through Diet*, Lon.: Methuen 1913 pp. 23-4

base for these tiny loaves, which were baked to a brown crustiness and eaten with our noon meal or taken on trips.

The main dish for supper was a really large salad, enough to provide at least one over-flowing bowl for each person. This salad was fruit or vegetable, depending on the garden resources. In a big wooden bowl we emulsified lemon or lime juice with rose-hip juice and olive oil, and into that cut peppers, celery, onion, radish, parsley, tomatoes, cucumbers, lettuce,—whatever was growing in the garden at the time. Sometimes we shredded raw beet, carrot, squash, celery root, turnip and made that a complete salad, with celery, nuts and raisins, lemon and oil. In winter, white or red cabbage was the bulk item instead of lettuce. To this we added cut up apples, nuts, oranges or grapefruit and celery. In summer we could add raw young peas, tips of asparagus, or fresh raw corn. We picked these salads just before making, and made them just before eating them. Thus the full vitamin content was retained. Supper could be planned and picked half an hour before meal-time, bespeaking "the infinite conveniences of what a well-stocked garden affords".[32] This "vernal pottage" was "ready at hand and easily dress'd; requiring neither Fire, Cost, or Attendance, to boil, roast, and prepare them as did Flesh and other provisions".[33] "The Huswife was never surpriz'd, had all at hand, and could in a Trice set forth an handsome Sallet."[34]

Some suppertimes we merely cleaned and washed the vege-tables; then put them, whole, in bowls on the center of the table and let folk serve themselves. There were many possibilities: lettuce hearts; escarolle, endive, dandelion and spinach leaves; cauliflower buds, brussels sprouts, sprigs of broccoli and parsley;

[32] John Evelyn, *Acetaria*, Lon.; Tooke 1699, p. 795
[33] *Ibid.*, p. 3
[34] *Ibid.*, p. 185

whole carrots, radishes, tomatoes and cucumbers; celery and asparagus stalks; young sweet corn, green peas and peppers. In fact, anything that would go into a salad could also be served completely uncut. The people at the table helped themselves and combined whatever specially appealed.

In winter before washing and cutting up the salad materials at suppertime, we put on potatoes or squash to bake. Squash, as well as potatoes, we baked whole, in the skin. The steam generated inside the skin tenderized the vegetables in record time and helped retain all the natural food values. When corn, asparagus, peas or beans were ripe in the garden we added them to our evening meal, cooking as short a time as possible, in as little water as possible. Years ago we got rid of all our aluminum kitchen ware, as we believe aluminum is more soluble than most metals and leaves a deposit in the pan which affects food adversely and probably acts as a slow poison in the human system. What little cooking we did was done in stainless steel or enamel or pottery or glass vessels.

All of our meals were eaten at a wooden plank table, in wooden bowls, the same bowl right through the meal. This practically eliminated the dish-washing problem. With no sauces, no frying and the like, there were few dishes to wash and pans to scrub. Our salad we ate with chop sticks, as we found the "nimble boys" (Chinese "fai-tze") more selective and discriminating in picking up food than the shovel-like fork. We also felt that wooden eating utensils were more neutral and modified the flavor less than the metallic table tools.

These food habits of ours we found simple, economical and practicable, though they were perhaps not usual for 20th century Americans. With advancing civilization, the American diet pattern, like everything else, has undergone a thorough-going change. The business of procuring the necessities of life has been shifted from the wood lot, the garden, the kitchen and the family to the factory and the large-scale enterprise. In our case, we moved our center back to the land. There we raised the food we ate. We found it sufficient, delicious and nourishing. On this diet we maintained a rugged health and patronized no doctors. Our "apothecary shop was the woods and fields".[35] "By attention to Diet, many diseases may be prevented, and others mitigated. It is a just observation that he who lives by rule and wholesome diet, is a physician to himself."[36] With vegetables, fruits, nuts and cereals we proved that one could maintain a healthy body as an operating base for a sane mind and a purposeful harmless life.

[35] Samuel Thomson, *New Guide to Health*, Boston: Adams 1835 p. 9
[36] Anon., *Concise Directions on the Nature of our Common Food so far as it tends to Promote or Injure Health*, Lon.: Swords 1790, p. 7

"It is true that to obtain money by trade is sometimes more profitable, were it not so hazardous; and likewise lending money at interest, if it were an honorable occupation."

Marcus Porcius Cato, De Agri Cultura, 149 B.C.

"The countrey-man hath a provident and gainfull familie, not one whose necessities must be alwaies furnished out of the shop, nor their table out of the market. His provision is alwaies out of his own store, and agreeable with the season of the yeare."

Don Antonio de Guevara, The Praise and Happiness of the Countrie-Life, 1539

"There is no man alive that affects a country life more than myself; no man it may be, who has more experienc'd the delices of it; but even those, without action, were intollerable."

John Evelyn, Public Employment Prefer'd to Solitude, 1667

"He certainly is worthy great Praise and Honour, who, possessing a large and barren Demesne, constrains it, by his Industry and Labour, to produce extra ordinary Plenty, not only to his own Profit, but that of the Public also."

Sir Richard Weston, Legacy to his Sons, 1759

"In our present imperfect condition, a beneficent Providence has not reserved a moderate success in Agriculture exclusively to the exercise of a high degree of intelligence. His laws have been so kindly framed, that the hand even of uninstructed toil may receive some requital in remunerating harvests; while their utmost fulness can be anticipated only where corporeal efforts are directed by the highest intelligence."

R. L. Allen, The American Farmers Book, 1849

"Who ever knew a good farmer, of prudent habits, to fail?"

John L. Blake, Farmer's Every-Day Book, 1850

"If a man would enter upon country life in earnest and test thoroughly its aptitudes and royalties, he must not toy with it at a town distance; he must brush the dews away with his own feet. He must bring the front of his head to the business, and not the back of it."

Donald G. Mitchell, My Farm of Edgewood, 1863

CHAPTER 6

ROUNDING OUT A LIVELIHOOD

Livelihood needs—Stability and security—The basis of our consumer economy—Liberation from city markets—The craftsman's competence—A no-money economy—Personal responsibility and foresight necessary for a livelihood

LIVELIHOOD is the central core around which most people build their lives. There are exceptions, of course. But the majority of human beings, notably in industrial communities, dedicate their best hours and their best years to getting an income and exchanging it for the necessaries and decencies of physical and social existence. Children, old people, the crippled, the sick, the voluntarily parasitic are at least partially freed from livelihood preoccupations. Able-bodied adults have little choice. They must meet the demands of livelihood or pay a heavy penalty in social disapproval, insecurity, anxiety and finally in physical hardship.

Livelihood needs, particularly for the necessities, are continuous, operating every day, of every month, of every year. An interruption in the supply of necessary goods and services, even for a short time, results in hardship and creates an atmosphere of uncertainty, insecurity, anxiety and fear. By what means are the stability and security of livelihood to be safeguarded?

Without going into a long discussion, we would suggest seven procedures which will maximize the stability and security of livelihood.

First, regulating the sources of livelihood in such a manner that all able-bodied adults will render a service in exchange for income, thus eliminating the social divisions which develop when a part of the community lives on unearned income while the remainder exchanges labor power for its livelihood.

Second, avoid gross and glaring inequalities in livelihood status.

Third, budget and plan the community economy.

Fourth, keep community books, and open the accounts to public inspection.

Fifth, pay as you go, either in labor or materials, thus avoiding inflation.

Sixth, practice economy, conserving resources, producing and consuming as little as necessary rather than as much as possible.

Seventh, provide a wide range of social services based upon specialization and cooperation.

All seven of these propositions deserve the careful attention of any one interested in rounding out a livelihood. Since livelihood is the subject matter of a previous book, *Economics for the Power Age,*[1] we have outlined its ingredients here only that we might have a background against which to discuss the methods which we followed in meeting the livelihood problem which faced us in Vermont.

It would have been quite possible to live in the Vermont hills as one did in the suburbs of New York or Boston, by going frequently to market in nearby towns, buying to meet all one's needs in shops, using fruits and vegetables loaded with poisonous

[1] Scott Nearing, N.Y.: John Day 1952

sprays and dusts and far removed from their production source, plus the processed and canned output of the food industry. Such a procedure was followed by several families in the valley, as long as they could afford it. Meanwhile they paid the usual price in lowered vitality and ill health.

We were not at all pulled in this direction, partly because we believed in fresh, vital food, organically produced, and partly because our economy was planned on the assumption that we would produce and use everything possible, relying upon cash-spending for the smallest residue of goods and services procured outside the circle of our household establishment.

The basis of our consumer economy was the garden. By raising and using garden products as outlined in the two previous chapters we were able to provide ourselves with around 80% of our food.[2] Shelter, which ranks next to food in the budget of the low-income household,[3] we provided by the system of construction described in the chapter on building a home. For fuel we used wood, cut on the place. Some of our neighbors heated with coal, oil, gas or electricity. We enjoyed work in the forest, which needed continual cleaning and weeding. And wood cut and used on the place necessitated no cash outlay, but represented a direct return for our labor. Thoreau said on cutting one's own fuel: "It warms us twice, and the first warmth is the most wholesome and memorable, compared with which the other is mere coke . . . The greatest value is received before the wood is teamed home."[4]

Our Vermont economy provided food, shelter and fuel, the big

[2] "Food represents nearly 40% of the budget of the average urban family." Ralph Borsodi, in *The Interpreter*, March 1, 1946, p. 2
[3] "Shelter represents, on the average, 25% of the total budget of those who pay rent in cities," *Ibid.*, p. 1
[4] *Journal*, 10/22/1853

items among necessaries,[5] mainly or entirely on a use basis. With rather wide limitations, we could have a supply of these things in direct proportion to the amount of labor time that we were willing to put into their production. Our purpose in going to Vermont however, was not to multiply food, housing, fuel and the other necessaries, but to get only enough of these things to meet the requirements of a living standard that would maintain our physical efficiency and at the same time provide us with sufficient leisure to pursue our chosen avocations. Livelihood was no end in itself,—rather it was a vestibule into an abundant and rewarding life. Therefore we produced the necessaries only to a point which would provide for efficiency. When we reached that point, we turned our attention and energies from bread labor to avocations or to social pursuits.

Current practice in United States economy called upon the person who had met his needs for necessaries to turn his attention forthwith to procuring comforts and conveniences, and after that to luxuries and superfluities. Only by such procedures could an economy based on profit accumulation hope to achieve the expansion needed to absorb additional profits and pay a return to those investing in the new industries.

Our practice was almost the exact opposite of the current one. Our consumer necessaries came mostly from the place, on a use basis. Comforts and conveniences came from outside the farm and had to be procured either by barter or through cash outlays. We bartered for some products,—chiefly food which we could not raise in a New England climate. Cash outlay meant earning additional cash income. Consequently, we endeavored to do as

[5] "A proper program of country living would, by providing food and shelter alone, make the average family secure with regard to approximately 60% of their needs." Borsodi, *Ibid.*, p. 2

Robert Louis Stevenson advised in his Christmas Sermon, "earn a little and spend a little less". Food from the garden and wood from the forest were the product of our own time and labor. We paid no rent. Taxes were reasonable. We bought no candy, pastries, meats, soft drinks, alcohol, tea, coffee or tobacco. These seemingly minor items mount up and occupy a large place in the ordinary family's budget. We spent little on clothes and knick-knacks. We lighted for fifteen years with kerosene and candles. We never had a telephone or radio. Most of our furniture was built in and hand made. We did our trading in town not more than twice in a month, and then our purchases were scanty.

"Civilization," said Mark Twain, "is a limitless multiplication of unnecessary necessaries." A market economy seeks by bally-hoo to bamboozle consumers into buying things they neither need nor want, thus compelling them to sell their labor power as a means of paying for their purchases. Since our aim was liberation from the exploitation accompanying the sale of labor power, we were as wary of market lures as a wise mouse is wary of other traps.

Readers may label such a policy as painfully austere, renuncia-tory or bordering on deliberate self-punishment. We had no such feeling. Coming from New York City, with its extravagant dis-plays of non-essentials and its extensive wastes of everything from food and capital goods to time and energy, we were surprised and delighted to find how much of the city clutter and waste we could toss overboard. We felt as free, in this respect, as a caged wild bird who finds himself once more on the wing. The demands and requirements which weigh upon city consumers no longer restricted us. To the extent that we were able to meet our con-sumer needs in our own way and in our own good time, we had freed ourselves from dependence upon the market economy.

Vermont life liberated us as consumers from the limitations, restrictions and compulsions of the city market. It had an even more profound effect upon us as producers. A household economy based on a maximum of self-sufficiency gives the householder a maximum of responsibility.

Householders living under a use economy must provide their own goods and services, not only in sufficient amount, but at the proper time. Dwellers in a remote valley cannot send or phone to the corner grocery an hour before supper. They must plan and prepare during the previous season. If radishes are to be ready for the table on the first of June, they must be planted not later than the first week in May. If seeds are to yield the best results, the soil must be prepared before the planting day. Soil preparation with us, necessitated compost. Compost piles, to be available in the Spring, had to be set up by mid-summer of the previous year. To enjoy fresh radishes on June 1, we began to get ready ten or twelve months in advance.

Similarly with the fuel supply. It is possible to burn green wood by putting it in the oven or under the stove and drying the outside fibres before the sticks go into the fire-box. They will not burn really well, but neither will they put the fire out. Best results are obtained by splitting the wood in the open, leaving it in a heap until sun and wind have seared over the outside, then piling it in an open-sided woodshed for six months. This means, in practice, that the winter's wood supply should be under cover by the previous spring. If the wood can be cut one year in advance, put under cover and burned the following year, so much the better.

Another example of necessary foresight can be taken from our building. There was a place in the lumber shed where cement was kept. Before taking a trip to town (fifteen miles to Manchester in one direction or thirty miles to Brattleboro in the other) we always looked at the cement stock, and if it was below five bags, we brought back another five or ten. In this way we usually had cement when it was needed. Otherwise the job would have been held up while we put in time and motion and money making a special trip to either town. Incidentally, by buying in ton lots, paying cash in advance and doing our own hauling from the lumber yard, we saved from five to ten cents on every bag of cement we used. By such devices much of our cement cost us as little as sixty cents a bag, and it was always ready at hand.

Isolated self-contained households meet their needs for current repairs and upkeep as they meet the requirements for capital installation, by keeping on hand a modest supply of lumber, hardware and simple tools and dealing with repairs and replacements at appropriate times. Such jobs, when completed, might not look professional, but they use the ingenuity and stretch the imagination of the householder and provide excellent training. After all is said and done, it is foolish and wasteful to let the professional building tradesman think out, plan, construct and at the end of the job thrill with the joy of work well done. "Shall we," asks Thoreau, "forever resign the pleasure of construction to the carpenter?"[6]

Power age economy has substituted the specialized machine and the assembly line for the craftsman, and has transformed many a skilled worker into a machine tender, with a resulting concentration, not upon excellence, but upon volume of product. The average city worker is asked to accept a wage or salary as a substitute for pride in workmanship and the satisfaction of mastery over tools and materials.

Our self-contained Vermont economy, with its dependence

[6] *Walden*, Boston: Ticknor & Fields 1854 p. 51

upon our own productive efforts, reopened for us a great variety of competences of which the average city dweller knows little. The most important group of these competences was associated with the use of the soil and the production and preparation of food. Building, equipping and repairing dwelling units, and the making and repairing of tools and implements presented us with a second sphere of productive functioning. Cutting logs and firewood and the clearing of woodland brought us into contact with forestry and its associated practices. In all of these fields we were compelled to think, plan, assemble materials and tools, and practice the techniques required to obtain the results we had in view.

City dwellers, accustomed to a wide variety of services, get to a point at which they believe that the essential questions of day to day living can be settled by arrangement, chiefly over a telephone. A customer with a ten dollar bill can get wonderful results in a department store. But put the same person in the backwoods with a problem to be solved and an inadequate supply of materials and tools. There money is useless. Instead, ingenuity, skill, patience and persistence are the coin current. The store customer, who comes home with a package under his arm has learned nothing, except that a ten dollar bill is a source of power in the market place. The man or woman who has converted material into needed products via tools and skills has matured in the process. A telephone call and a charge account get results in a market center. Very different requirements are called into play in a household aiming at maximum self-sufficiency.

The school of hard knocks is merciless. One can argue with a storekeeper, a taxi driver or even with a traffic officer. A square, a level, a bit of knotty pine, a badly mixed batch of concrete, a leaky pipe or a short circuit are implacable. There they stand, pointing the finger of accusation at the careless or the ignorant or clumsy worker. If, under such conditions, one knows good work and wants it, there is only one thing to do,—tear out the job and begin all over again.

Self-contained rural economies require a certain amount of cash with which to pay taxes, to buy hardware and tools, and in our case to purchase clothing, which we never attempted to produce during our stay in Vermont. The city man who has learned to depend on a wage or salary feels a sense of uncertainty, bordering on terror, when he contemplates weeks, months and years minus a pay check. Where, he asks, is the money coming from?

George Breen, when he came into the valley from Connecticut, had been a salesman for so many years that he could not imagine what it would be like to live a week without a pay check. He stepped into the situation warily, as a man approaches any unknown country, filled with misgivings and a sense of real insecurity. We felt a bit the same way when we plunged from the whirlpool of New York life into the tranquillity of hills and forests. Money was the coin of the urban realm from which we came,—the open sesame to the satisfaction of needs and wants. When we left the city, we felt we had left cash payment behind. When it reared its ugly head even in the Vermont wilderness, we kept it in its place and made it our business to see only that there was a surplus of receipts over expenditures. William Cooper, in his *Guide in the Wilderness* said wisely, "It is not large funds that are wanted, but a constant supply, like a small stream that never dies. To have a great capital is not so necessary as to know how to manage a small one and never to be without a little."[7]

[7] Dublin: Gilbert & Hodges 1810 pp. 53-6

Aside from public education, poor relief, old age pensions and the social security taxes and payments which gradually entered the life of rural Vermont between 1932 and 1952, the stability and security of a household depended upon its internal balance, upon the health of its members and their willingness to work or otherwise contribute toward the goods and services upon which household survival depended.

Houses in our section were well kept or disorderly, neat or squalid and run down, in proportion to the willingness of the adult family members to put time and energy into the multiple tasks that must be performed before neatness and order can be established and maintained. "Many a farm of ample acreage is left to the rheumatic labor of advancing decrepitude. . . There is no strength for repairs, no ambition for improvement, and no expectation of more than a bare subsistence . . . It only requires courage, a cold shoulder to croakers, energy, skill and application."[8]

Virtually every family in the valley had some kind of garden, which was planted in the spring, tended perfunctorily during the summer, and neglected and abandoned to weeds by the fall.

The valley bordered The Wilderness of which Stratton Mountain was the center. Wild life abounded. Deer were so numerous that at times they made gardening all but impossible, yet throughout the valley there were few garden fences. The natives preferred to have their gardens near the house, keep dogs and cats, and take chances.

Rainfall was around 45 inches per year, fairly well distributed through the seasons, but almost every summer there were minor

[8] "Farming in New England", *Report of Commissioner of Agriculture,* Wash. D.C.: Gov. Printing Office 1871 p. 255

droughts, and periodically rainless spells dried cultivated fields
to powder. The valley abounded in springs and streams; there
were stones everywhere and sand and gravel for the taking. Yet
no family built an irrigation tank or the beginnings of an irrigation system.

Garden land sloped, much of it steeply, yet the valley was
terraceless. During our two decades in the valley we never saw
an example of contour farming, ridging or drainage.

Buildings throughout the valley were poor, many being roofed
with wood shingles, involving a high fire risk. Most places did
not have water running into the house, nor did they have so
much as a rain barrel of water stored against fire during a dry
period. To be. sure, in the last twenty years, only one house
burned down in the valley, but chimney fires were frequent and
an adequate fire department miles away.

Of paper work,—planning, budgeting, book-keeping, there
was little. Most families spent what they had, ran into debt and
hoped for the best. "There is not a single step in the life of a
farmer that does not prove the advantage of his keeping regular
accounts; and yet there is not one in a thousand who does it."[9]

We never expected to devote more than half of our time to
bread labor, but during that time we took the livelihood problem
seriously. We had some training in agriculture and forestry, in
civil, mechanical and social engineering. We dealt with the
entire livelihood problem in the same way that we faced problems
in any of these fields. There are accepted techniques, in science
as well as in technology. We attempted to apply the principles
and practices of science and technology to the problems we encountered in rounding out a semi-subsistence livelihood. We
surveyed the problem at hand, thought about it, discussed it,

[9] Arthur Young, *The Farmer's Calendar*, Lon.: Phillips 1805 p. 569

made plans, assembled the needed materials and tools, and then proceeded to work out solutions, in terms of the particular situation. Hence, we fenced, irrigated, terraced, planned, constructed, marking ourselves as odd, queer, over-ambitious and perhaps even a trifle un-neighborly by setting up standards of performance which were far removed from those accepted and followed by the neighborhood.

"That every Man should imploy him self not only for the advancing of his own Interest, but likewise that he may propogate the Wellfare of others will, I suppose, be sooner granted than practised. . . . It is necessary, that some be imployed one way, and some another, So that each may attain to some Competent Degree of Knowledge of, and Dexterity in the Vocation or imployment he Professes, So that every One may be Useful and Assisting to another, And by a mutual Good Correspondence with one another, all may live Comfortable together."

James Donaldson, The Undoubted Art of Thriving, 1700

"Oh, knew he but his happiness, of men
The happiest he! who far from public rage,
Deep in the vale, with a choice few retir'd,
Drinks the pure pleasures of the Rural Life."

James Thomson, The Seasons, 1730

"These countrymen in general are a very happy people; they enjoy many of the necessities of life upon their own farms, and what they do not so gain, they have from the sale of their surplus products: it is remarkable to see such numbers of these men in a state of great ease and content, possessing all the necessaries of life, but few of the luxuries of it. Their farms yield food—much of cloathing—most of the articles of building—with a surplus sufficient to buy such foreign luxuries as are necessary to make life passably comfortable: there is very little elegance among them —but more of necessaries."

Anonymous, American Husbandry, 1775

"Thrice happy days! In rural business passed:
Blest winter nights! when, as the genial fire
Cheers the wide hall, his cordial family
With soft domestic arts and hours beguilt . . .
Sometimes, at eve,
His neighbors lift the latch, and bless unbid
His festal roof; while, o'er the light repast,
And sprightly cups, they mix in social joy;
And, through the maze of conversation, trace
Whate'er amuses or improves the mind."

John Armstrong, The Art of Preserving Health, 1838

"My most serene irresponsible neighbors, let us see that we have the whole advantage of each other; we will be useful, at least, if not admirable, to one another."

Henry Thoreau, A Week on the Concord and Merrimack Rivers, 1849

"We have learned to be chary of roads; they mean people, and commotion, and lack of peace."

Herbert Jacobs, We Chose the Country, 1948

CHAPTER 7

LIVING IN A COMMUNITY

The neighbors look us over—We prefer cooperation to wage labor—Successful and unsuccessful neighborhood group effort—With cooperative effort the valley could have thrived—Insufficient interest and enthusiasm—Community social affairs—The Community House—Individualism rampant—A musical hour—One successful communal effort

WE WENT to Vermont as outsiders. Natives in those parts frequently use the word "foreigners" to describe newcomers. In view of the suspicion they feel and their reluctance to admit outsiders into their neighborhood circle they should call them "interlopers."

Every community demands conformity to its laws, expects the acceptance of its customs and folkways, and prefers to have none but native sons at its firesides. In small remote communities this preference tends to take precedence over all other considerations. In 1932, depression hardship was felt even in our Green Mountain wilderness. Vernet Slason, a native of Londonderry, five miles north of Bondville, married a Bondville girl, Eva Crowninshield, and settled down there. He was handy at carpenter work and painting; fixed up a saw-rig and cut cordwood for neighbors, and quickly made himself a place in the work life of the town. One of the old Bondvillites reacted to this incursion with the comment, "I don't see why these outsiders should come in here and take work away from our boys."

If a native-born Vermonter elicited such a response by moving across some hills and settling down in a nearby valley, imagine the reception given to people born in other states, who emigrated to the town of Winhall, Vermont, direct from New York City. Here was an immense barrier to surmount. We looked upon association with the community as a necessary aspect of the good life. How were we to be accepted? We were law-abiding citizens for the most part, but we did not conform to the folkways and we were not native sons.

When we first arrived, the neighbors looked us over. In less than no time they knew the minutest details about us,—where we came from, what we had been doing there, how old we were, what kind of a car we drove, its condition and performance, the kind of clothes we wore, the food we ate and a hundred other items.

One of our first steps in Vermont was to ask the Lightfoots, who were our nearest neighbors and lived less than a quarter of a mile away, whether they would supply us with milk. They agreed, and one or another of the Lightfoot girls would come over each day and deliver it. Sometimes all three brought it over. There was a much-worn woodbox with a big hinged cover, in the kitchen of our house. There the three little girls would perch like birds in a row—Minnie, the oldest, with her feet just reaching the floor; Mary, with her legs dangling, and Gladys, who must have been about four or five, with her legs sticking straight out in front of her. With their big solemn eyes, they saw everything, remembered everything and doubtless gave their reports to playmates and home-folks.

Our ways amused the neighbors, baffled them or annoyed them. Perhaps the most consistent and emphatic disapproval was directed against our diet. We could more easily have been accepted if we had eaten in the approved way. We ate from wooden bowls, with chopsticks, not from china plates, with forks and spoons; we ate food raw that, according to Vermont practices, should have been cooked, and we cooked weeds and outlandish things that never should be eaten at all. That we ate no meat was in itself strange; but during our entire twenty years in Vermont we never baked a pie, we seldom ate cake or cookies and almost never doughnuts. In a community which serves pie, cake and doughnuts for two if not three meals a day, conduct such as ours was not only unbelievable but reprehensible. We simply failed to live up to the accepted Vermont pattern.

To the credit of Vermont conservatism it must be said that during the two decades of our stay, after innumerable discussions and long-drawn-out arguments on the subject of white flour, white bread, white sugar, pies and pastries, the necessity for eating raw vegetables, and the revolting practice of consuming decaying animal carcasses, no native Vermont family of our acquaintance made any noticeable change in its food habits.

We desired to get on with our neighbors, but we were not willing to conform to their patterns of living and they would not adopt ours. So we agreed to differ and made allowances for each other's idiosyncrasies. They abode by their traditions and we planned and lived our lives un-Vermontishly.

We had much to learn, and some of our ideas were not well adapted to Vermont.[1] For instance, when it came to culverts, which clog up with leaves and brush during the wet season and

[1] "It would seem that the gentleman ought to serve an apprenticeship with some dirt farmer, before he embarked on his own account, in a business with which he is entirely unacquainted." John Lorain, *The Practise of Husbandry,* Phil.: Carey 1825 p. 404

make no end of trouble,—we put in stone-paved, open fords such as we had seen in Washington's Rock Creek Park. The neighbors assured us that these fords would not work in winter because the water would take out the snow at the center of the ford, leaving two high snow banks on either side which would have to be broken down before the road could be used. We persisted in building several of the fords and the neighbors turned out to be right. Furthermore, some of the stones at the edge of the fords were heaved by frost and made additional trouble. We gave up ford building, and the neighbors snorted with satisfaction: "We told you so."

On the issue of concrete stacks, however, we made our point. Vermont sap houses are equipped with galvanized iron stacks. Our evaporator called for a stack 22 inches in diameter and 28 feet high. It came in six foot sections which were bulky and about all one man cared to handle, even on the ground. Traditionally, the stack was erected at the beginning of the sap season. It took several adults to handle the job. The lower sections were easy; the higher ones difficult and dangerous. At the end of the sap season, careful operators took the stack down and stored it, careless folk left it up to rust until the next season.

After mounting and dismounting the stack for two or three years we decided to put up a permanent one. We discussed brick, but finally chose concrete, using our old galvanized stack as the inside form and constructing a square outside form in sections, bolted in place, and moved up as we built. The sap house was already constructed, with concrete foundations and a concrete floor, so we put the stack outside the sap house and connected it through an opening in the galvanized wall. After some minor obstacles had been overcome, we completed the stack and the next sap season, tried it out. It drew well. So far as we know, this was the first concrete stack attached to a Vermont sugarhouse. It has stood in place, without repairs of any kind, for some fifteen years. Instead of laboriously and dangerously erecting a galvanized stack every spring, two men working twenty minutes, inserted a galvanized section between the stack and the evaporator, and we were ready to boil sap.

Building a concrete stack led to plenty of neighborhood comment. Ruth Hamilton, one of the neighbors, who would be rated even by Vermonters as a conservative, came up to have a look at the stack in operation. She had made syrup for years and knew all the techniques. After watching for a time she turned to a bystander with the approving remark: "Well, they may be socialists but they do have good ideas."

That qualified endorsement was one of the warmest that we got in the neighborhood. Many other comments were far less flattering. Even the neighbors who liked us were sceptical about most of our queer ways.

We were cooperators in theory and were anxious to put the theory into practice. From the beginning we worked with our neighbors, sometimes on their side of the fence, sometimes on our side. We disapprove of the wage relation on principle and if we could avoid it by cooperative exchange of labor we would never enter into it in practice. The purchase and sale of labor power is not a healthy social relationship and we far prefer a fair and equal exchange of time or of products. On every possible occasion we turned to cooperation and mutual aid. When necessary, we compromised on wage labor, but we held it to a minimum, and always on the neighbor's terms. In any such transaction we discussed the work to be done and then said: "How much will you expect for that job?" Or else, after the job was completed, we asked "How much do we owe you?" Never once did we have any reason to question or hesitate to pay what was asked.

The relationships which we enjoy most can be illustrated by the deal we made with one neighboring family who wanted a fireplace. Alice and Chuck Vaughan had bought an old farm-house, a dozen miles from our place, and were turning it into a ski lodge. The local masons wanted $600 to build a brick fireplace and chimney. We suggested that the Vaughans build it themselves but they had never tackled such a job and were a bit wary. At that time we were building a set of stone steps up a boulder-face to a cabin in the woods. It was heavy work and we could use help. We talked the matter over with them and made the following arrangement. They would put in their fireplace foundation to floor level. We would work with them on the fireplace and carry the chimney to the peak of the roof. We figured this would take us six working days. They, in exchange, would put in six working days on our stone steps, and on some canning.

The plan worked out nicely. At the cost of twelve days harmonious sociable work (plus their work on the foundation) they got a fireplace, with no cash outlay except for materials, which they would have had to buy in any case. We, on our side, got an equivalent amount of help with our heavy stone steps and our canning.

Such relationships are sound economically,—an exchange from which both parties gain, without exploitation on either side. Socially, they are based on the equalitarian principle of exchanging labor time. Each puts in an equal number of hours and does his best according to his abilities. Thoreau says in *Walden*: "If a man has faith, he will cooperate with equal faith everywhere; if he has not faith, he will continue to live like the rest of the world, whatever company he is joined to. To cooperate in the highest as well as the lowest sense, means to get our living together."[2]

A few other of our neighbors were cooperators in theory. Most of them were indifferent, or actively hostile to it. When the theoretical cooperators found that cooperation began with planning, and succeeded only in so far as the cooperators stuck to the plans, assumed responsibility for their fulfilment, and then lived up to their obligations, most of them thought better of it and went back to the individualistic pattern of "everyone for himself and on his own."[3]

The attitude is well illustrated by Harold Field's reaction to our rationalized methods of syrup production. Harold is an amiable, ingenious inventor and a painstaking workman when he once gets going. In theory he believes in cooperation; in practice he likes to go to bed when he makes up his mind to it and to get up and work when he feels like it. He sugared with us one year and found there were disadvantages. During the syrup making season we were extra careful to keep on schedule because so much depended on picking up the sap as soon as it was in the buckets and getting it into the evaporator before it began to ferment.

Harold had a sugar grove of sorts, but his trees were fairly small and many of them were soft maple, not superior producers. He had no sugarhouse. So we made an arrangement whereby Harold would sugar with us, contribute his own time and that of his team, some sap buckets and other tools, in exchange for a specified percentage of the syrup crop, to be shared with him on

[2] Boston: Ticknor & Fields 1854 p. 78
[3] "There are some People that care for none of these Things, that will enter into no new Scheme, not take up any other Business than what they have been enured to, unless you can promise Mountains of Gold." Jared Eliot, *Essays*, Boston: Edes & Gill 1760 p. 135

a day-to-day basis. The season was a good one and Harold ended it with around 150 gallons of syrup in exchange for about six weeks of work.

Harold was more than satisfied by the amount of syrup he got, but he felt that the work routine was too rigid. Besides, he reasoned, if that much syrup could be made with such a small outlay of effort, why should he not use his own trees, set up his own sugarhouses and have all the proceeds for himself? The next sap season therefore found Harold setting up his own sugar establishment and trying to do the job virtually single-handed. Syrup-making asks for division of labor and a considerable degree of coordination of effort. The most efficient tapping team, for instance, consists of three or four people. Gathering sap is one occupation, and boiling it down another. These operations should be performed at the same time, especially in mild weather, so that the sap does not stand around and sour. Harold had some difficult, harried seasons before he gave up syrup making on the argument that it did not pay him the going rate of day wages for the time he put in on it.

Zoe and Floyd Hurd were the people who first taught us how to make maple syrup. From 1933 to 1940 we sugared with them. Floyd and his family were Seventh Day Adventists. Believing that Saturday and not Sunday was the divinely ordained day of rest, neighborhood Adventists refused to work on Saturday or to do business that day. They would milk and water their cattle on Saturday and perform other urgent chores. If a neighbor insisted, they would let him have the necessaries of life, such as milk or eggs. Frequently, however, they would not take the money for these supplies until another day.

Walter Twing, one of the Seventh Day leaders in our neighborhood, had a pit in which there was clean and evenly-graded building sand. He was accommodating and always went out of his way to be friendly, but he would not let us take sand from his place on Saturday. Walter was one of the best sugar makers in the valley. He began extra early in the spring, emptied his buckets more frequently than most, made extra fine quality syrup and sugar, and always aimed to have the first sugar to carry to town meeting day, early in March. There is a tradition in the valley that at the height of his religious zeal Walter went among his maples on Friday at sundown, emptied the sap buckets, set them upside down and left them thus until Saturday's sunset, so that he would not use the sap which might drop on the Lord's day.

Zoe and Floyd were not so strict as Walter Twing. When we first worked with them they were willing to gather sap any day it ran. Later, however, they had some misfortunes which they attributed to their failure to observe the Sabbath. Both decided that, come what may, they would go to church Saturdays and would do no work. This decision, made early in the sap season, was followed by a series of week-ends in which sap started Friday, ran like mad all Saturday, and by Saturday night was overflowing the buckets.

Zoe and Floyd stuck to their principles and let the sap run and went to church. We had no such inhibitions, so we gathered the sap and boiled it down, on Saturday. Then came the crucial question: did the Hurds want to take their share of the syrup which had been made on the Sabbath, from sap that had run and been gathered that day? After debating the issue earnestly, they took their share of the syrup.

Had efforts to establish cooperation and mutual aid succeeded, a collective economy would have been a significant aspect of community activity. While several members of the valley population believed in the theory of cooperation, there was no deep concern to cooperate and no common push in that direction.

The valley in which we lived was designed by nature as an isolated, self-contained economic and social unit and would have thriven on collective undertakings. Five miles west of Jamaica, on the Pikes Falls road, the steep-sided canyon which carried a branch of the West River opened out into a valley half a mile wide by two miles long, running roughly from east to west. On the south loomed Stratton Mountain. On the north was Pinnacle Mountain. Access east and west was blocked by high hills, with half a dozen streams running through steep defiles across the bottom land and down to the West River. The entire valley of perhaps a thousand acres, plus wooded upland of another three or four thousand, did not contain enough good land for one first-class dairy farm. It was too high (1500 to 2000 feet above sea level) for most fruit. Three times in twenty years, July and August frosts trimmed squash, tomatoes, corn and even potato tops. Aside from the bottom land, flooded with every run-off of rain or melting snow, there was hardly a five acre piece that could be plowed without danger of severe erosion damage. The grazing season was short. Often snow lay from Thanksgiving to Easter.

On the other hand, there were eleven sugar groves in the valley, besides thousands of hard maples which had never been tapped. The surrounding hills carried millions of board feet of spruce, fir, hemlock, hard maple, yellow birch, white ash, basswood, beech, soft maple and poplar. Forest reproduction was automatic and forest growth was rapid. Given this set-up, it would have been possible (1) to erect a community saw-mill, saw out the necessary lumber and build or rebuild fifteen to twenty houses on appropriate pieces of land; (2) provide each dwelling unit with land for garden, fruit and outbuildings; (3) set up a central dairy unit to serve the entire valley; (4) maintain a central machine shop, carpenter shop, greenhouse unit and garage; (5) attach to the sawmill a wood-working plant which would convert the output of the scientifically forested timberland into toys or some other marketable wood product; (6) make maple syrup cooperatively, build a central packing house, put maple syrup and sugar into fancy packs and market them as opportunity offered; (7) supplement valley cash income by making hooked or braided rugs, carving wood, blacksmithing, making furniture, setting up a local school, a library and reading room, a social center and all facilities and activities necessary for a rounded life in the local community. Such an organization, well managed, and supported by the enthusiasm and idealism of the inhabitants, would have provided a livelihood and a reasonably satisfactory social life for 75 to 100 people. This would have been possible only on the basis of a common purpose, coordination, strong discipline and an iron will to see the project through over a period of at least a decade.

Plenty of young idealists drifted through the valley, staying for days, weeks, months and even years. To none did these ideas appeal sufficiently so that they were willing to take a hand and do something about it. Despite much talk and many meetings and discussions, no such cooperative unit was established. A few sporadic starts were made but no scheme was ever carried out to a successful conclusion.

The result was that an occasional itinerate saw mill, brought in for brief periods by professional lumbermen, made away with the standing timber. During our years in the valley we saw millions of feet of logs and lumber trucked out to Londonderry, Jamaica and Newfane. On the average, less than half of the sugar groves were tapped in any given year. Most of the syrup went in barrels to wholesale buyers, for a small return. Several attempts were made to do local bread-baking, but they were neither systematic nor long-lived. Almost equally unsuccessful were the efforts to organize a nursery school and kindergarten.

Literally scores of families, many with quite young children, visited the valley with the idea of locating there. A few of these tried it out for longer or shorter periods. At the end of twenty years, the valley population totalled a little less than it did at the beginning of our sojourn, and the degree of cooperation was limited to random swaps of products and services, with occasional examples of mutual aid in the handling of sickness or the care of young children, which would go on in any ordinary community in any part of the world.

The valley was inhabited by Vermonters and outsiders trained to private enterprise and, for the most part, rejects from private enterprise economy. Most of these men and women treasured their freedom as individuals and looked upon cooperative enterprise as the first step toward super-imposed discipline and coercion. They were suspicious of organized methods and planning. They would have none of it. Consequently, most community projects dealt only with leisure-time activities,—diversion or recreation.

These social affairs played an important part in the life of the valley. Despite the absence of a common economy, there was a persistent endeavor to organize neighborhood get-togethers at several different levels. "As Recreation is most necessary, so to none is it more due than to the Husbandman; . . . every toyl exacting some time for Recreation."[4]

In the early days, community affairs were held outdoors during

<hr>

[4] Gervase Markham, *Country Contentments*, Lon.: Sawbridge 1675 p. 2

the summer and early autumn. There were picnics at Pikes Falls and at different homes, marshmallow roasts, husking bees, house-raising bees, dancing parties. Outdoor meetings were fine in daylight or warm weather but some other arrangements obviously had to be made to meet storms and cold. Our stone-floored pine-panelled livingroom could accommodate almost forty people on couches, chairs and cushions, before a crackling fire. For several years it was used as an assembly point for discussions on world affairs and philosophical and other questions. These meetings usually took place on Saturday or Sunday evenings.

There was also a forum group in West Townshend, about 15 miles to the east of us, which held meetings on Wednesday evenings. The valley meetings seldom attracted more than thirty people. Attendance at the West Townshend Forum ran as high as a hundred on special occasions. Sometimes people from West Townshend came up to our meetings; frequently a dozen or more from our valley went down to theirs.

War tension in the early years, associated with the war of 1939–45, and later the passions roused by the cold war and the Korean war, put obstacles in the way of effective meetings. With few exceptions native Vermonters refused to attend the discussions both in our valley and in West Townshend on the ground that they were too radical. This was not surprising in view of the fact that the Vermonters, Republicans almost to a man, looked upon Democrats as way to the left. During the early years of the West Townshend Forum, high school students were encouraged by the local liberal principal to come from Leland and Grey Academy, five miles distant. Students also came from the nearby Newton School in Windham. As tension increased, students ceased attending the forums. In centers of population and with competent, experienced leaders, discussion groups are difficult to maintain over long periods even in peacetime. Discussion groups in wartime, in small, isolated communities, present still graver problems.

There were two main interest groups in the valley. One was concerned with world affairs and the meaning and purpose of life. The other wished to deal with strictly local matters and recreation,—the care of children, the organization of a nursery school, square dancing and the construction of a community house adequate to house these and similar undertakings. Attempts were made to alternate meetings on world affairs, local problems and recreation. Increased war tensions were reflected in the conflicting attitudes of valley folks. Eventually discussions were dropped and entertainment held the field.

Early in the development of valley community affairs, suggestions were made that a community center be established. Attempts to secure a local schoolhouse, belonging to the Jamaica School authorities, were unsuccessful. Norman Williams met the situation by buying an abandoned lumber camp, standing on forty acres of accessible land, and turning it over, under a deed of trust, to be used as a community center. After the place had been cleaned up and repaired, it was available for recreation and social gatherings.

From the time he came into the valley, Norm stood for a high degree of equalitarianism. He was disturbed because the local people remained aloof from community activities. Norm believed that "true community" was impossible unless all of the neighbors joined. In order to secure their participation, he argued, it was necessary to carry on activities in which all would be glad and willing to participate. In other words, activities were to be levelled down to the lowest common denominator.

Since experience had proved that the native Vermonters would not attend discussion groups, it was necessary to develop other more inclusive community undertakings. Norm believed that picnics, suppers and dances would fill the bill. The refitted community house was used for these purposes. With accordions and phonograph records and some amateur assistance, square dancing and folk dancing were developed to such a point that teams of dancers from the valley were invited to surrounding towns to give exhibitions. Square dances were held Saturday nights. So successful were they that people came for miles to take part in them. Still, everyone in the valley did not attend the Saturday night affairs. Furthermore, a new complication arose,—the use of liquor.

Soft drinks had been served or sold at the dances from the beginning in the community center. As attendance at the dances increased, people came who had been drinking. Others brought liquor and drank on the premises during the dances. There was brawling in one instance. Richard Gregg, Orpha Collie and Nelson Rawson, who were trustees of the community center at that time, posted a notice forbidding the use of liquor in the center. This brought the issue to a head. A community meeting was held. The trustees resigned. As their successors, three men were elected, all of whom favored the use of liquor on community house premises during dances. The trustees who had resigned were all at or past middle age. The new trustees were all members of the younger pre-middle age generation.

The liquor issue shook the community to its foundations. The decision to permit the use of liquor in the community center was thoroughly threshed out. There was no question but that the majority of the community favored freedom for drinkers and drinking. The anti-liquor minority refused to attend functions at the center if liquor was permitted.

Several issues involving morals and ethics had faced the community and had been settled or laid on the table without serious disruptive results except for the individuals concerned. The liquor question divided the community and proved so divisive that it caused the ultimate liquidation of the whole community house project. At one point there had been much talk of rebuilding the community house, so that it would include a craft center, school facilities and room for enlarged recreational activities. The controversy over alcohol drinking knocked the plans into a cocked hat.

This experience underlined the oft-repeated generalization that ideological agreement is an indispensable pre-requisite for the establishment of a successful cooperative group. Unity on objectives and on techniques is not enough, and even that was not in evidence in our valley. The community which desires to survive must have an ideology which is accepted by all of its members. The community house might have been a unifying factor of considerable importance in the life of the valley. Instead, almost through inadvertence, it underscored an element of discord which has played havoc with many an individual life and many a social group.

Throughout the entire effort to achieve valley-wide cooperation, each household remained an independent economic and social unit, with minor features of give and take maintained by special arrangement between the families involved. When the cycle was completed and the community house was abandoned, the valley stood about where it had been a decade earlier. There were recreational get-togethers now and again, but instead of valley-wide cooperation, animosities, family feuds and ideological antagonisms threaded through the entire life of the community.

Certainly this is not a pretty picture, nor does it offer hope to the many individuals and groups that have been looking and working toward the establishment in North America of cooperative communes or intentional communities of work. Perhaps the most significant lesson of the experience is that human beings, conditioned from birth by the professions and practices of a private enterprise, individualistic pattern have little more chance to cooperate effectively than a leopard has to change his spots.

War-time pressures and the sharp differences of viewpoint which were frequently expressed during our discussions of public questions, plus our own inclinations, led us to try out another experiment looking to community integration,—a musical hour each Sunday morning. During the open season, weather permitting, we held the musical session on a back terrace of the house, under the trees; in rough weather, before the fire in our livingroom.

The affair was very informal. At 10:30 whoever was on hand began taking part. The program itself was put together in terms of the interests and capacities of those present. Because of the wide diversity of religious and anti-religious views in the valley, it was necessary not to stress nor yet to avoid musical compositions of a religious nature. With minor exceptions we crossed this hurdle successfully. Rounds and folktunes were always possible. Singers who could tackle more ambitious part-songs were not always present but were eagerly sought. If no one came from outside the immediate household, which was occasionally the case in bad weather, the phonograph or organ was played.

For regularly attended sessions the music period was divided roughly into two parts,—*amateur* singing or instrument performances, and *professional* music from records,—unless we were fortunate enough to have present professional vocalists or instrumentalists. If people came who could perform musically or who had pronounced musical tastes, the program shifted ac-cordingly. At one time a good violinist dropped in and played for us to organ accompaniment; a guitarist came who picked out Bach themes on his strings; at another time a woman with an out-standing voice happened by who delighted us with her deep, full tones. We took advantage of any talent. One notable Sunday a professional flautist and two recorder players appeared from nowhere, a quintet was organized and put in four solid hours working through a pile of ensemble music. Time was barely taken out to eat and then back to the music. These artists dropped in by chance and we never saw them again.

The music hour proved to be a community success. More people came to it than attended discussions of public questions. When the music was over, they visited together, looked over our garden or the house and usually departed with arms or boxes filled with vegetables or flowers. As far as we could judge, they got more from music than from discussions. Certainly antagon-ism and bitterness were almost entirely absent from our musical sessions.

One notable event did bring the valley together,—the cancel-lation of the mail route in 1945. The war was on and gasoline was rationed. We were deep in the snows of a heavy winter. Cars were few and the young men to drive them were mostly overseas. Old folks particularly were hard put to it to get to town, and Wallace Crowninshield, the local mailman, kept them in touch with the outer world by bringing and taking the mail three times a week, plus occasional help with needed groceries and other provisions. At this critical juncture, with only a week's notice, the Post Office Department in Washington ordered the rural mail route discontinued, on the ground that the service did not pay its way.

People in the valley were shocked and stunned, and then, as the full import of this decision dawned on them—angry. Talk back and forth crystallized almost immediately into action. A volunteer committee secured the use of the local schoolhouse, contacted all who depended on the mail route, and called a meeting to decide on a course of action. The meeting was held on a snowy night in February. The valley people struggled through the drifts. Several groups came in from nearby Jamaica and Bondville. By meeting-time, the schoolhouse was crowded with forty-odd men, women and children. The stove was cherry red; the two school oil lamps and several lanterns dimly lighted up the faces of natives and newcomers alike. During our whole time in the valley we never saw so representative a gathering,— not even at a funeral. Uncle Sam's abrupt cancellation of the mail route had brought the entire community together in a move to get back the R.F.D.

The meeting elected Charles McCurdy chairman; Helen Nearing, secretary, with Jack Lightfoot, Raymond Styles and Scott Nearing to act as advisers of "The Pikes Falls Citizens Committee." Strategy was discussed and provision was made for rounding up all possible help and sympathy in getting the cancellation order rescinded. Our program was simple. All present were asked to write to the Postmaster General first of all, protesting the unfairness of his decision, next to our Senators and Representatives, notifying them of the situation and of our ire, and demanding their help. Letters were to be sent to the boys at the front, telling them to protest this cutting off of mail to and from their folks.

We planned letters to the local newspapers, but before we got them written, came a body blow from the *Brattleboro Reformer,* which said editorially that Pikes Falls was a nice little place to go fishing in the spring and summer but that the government was hardly justified in running a mail route for a mere fourteen families. This raised a howl from our little valley and some indignant letters to the paper. After printing them, the *Reformer* reversed its stand and said that instead of our puny Tuesday, Thursday, Saturday mail delivery we should be given daily service, with trolley car service and electric lights to boot. From then on, the *Brattleboro Reformer* was on our side in the fight and printed some twenty notices, letters and articles on the Pikes Falls mail route issue.

Another nearby paper, the *Bennington Banner,* started off with an editorial scoffing at the pretensions of a handful of little people back in the hills. Why, said the Editor, these folks have much greater advantages today than their like had a hundred years ago; the trouble with them is they've been educated to expect that by turning a spigot plenty of what they want will gush forth. That was going a little far. Both Brattleboro and Bennington had city water supplies; the comparison was offensive to people who carried their own water, from well or spring. These towns were our shopping towns and they were sneering at the countryside which brought them their business. We wrote our opinion of such tactics.

We came across a timely clipping from the *New York Times* which was brought to the attention of all and sundry. The issue of February 22, 1945 reported that the Post Office Department "expects an operating surplus of $265,214,280 in the next fiscal year." The gross annual cost of our mail route was less than $800. The big boys in Washington were saving dollars by taking pennies away from little people whose sons were at the front, fighting democracy's battles.

What a situation,—a handful of hill folk, isolated in a remote valley by a New England winter, their provincial need overshadowed by war, and their young men at the front,—entering a contest with the Government of the United States of North America. It was a case of David versus Goliath; a mouse attacking an elephant. The odds were against us, but we know who won in the Bible story and we had heard of mice putting elephants to flight.

We hired the Jamaica Town Hall and put on a well-attended meeting. Minutes were read of the first meeting, telling how the whole situation arose. Speeches from the floor were made, by children, by farm women whose sons were in the Pacific, by a soldier, John Stark, home on leave, by Frederick Van de Water, representing Freeman, Inc., who were currently engaged in a drive to prevent the Army engineers from constructing a dam that would flood the West River Valley. Resolutions were adopted and sent to the Postmaster General, to the Governor and to our Congressman and Senators. The meeting was lively and spontaneous. It was many a year since the neighborhood had been so stirred up and excited.

Response to this meeting was immediate. The Rutland and Burlington papers came to our support with articles. Headlines flared: "Pikes Falls Asks Senate Inquiry"; "Restoration of Mail Service Demanded at Mass Meeting". The Hon. Charles A. Plumley, member of Congress from Vermont, made a statement in the House of Representatives on Feb. 21st dealing with the rural service throughout the nation. After saying that he noticed that the Post Office Department was doing business at a profit and had accumulated a surplus of millions, he stated that its motto should be "service" not "profit". "The fact is the Department by rule of thumb is consolidating rural free delivery routes, suspending them, abolishing them all over the country to save money when they have a surplus, and at a time when the patrons anxiously await the arrival of a letter from their boys and girls in the service, which letter is never delivered." (Apparently Representatives do read the letters from their constituents.)

During the first week of the mail-route discontinuance a photographer and a reporter from the *Boston Globe* told the David-Goliath story to New England ("Vermont Hamlet Aroused by R.F.D. Discontinuance"). The second week, the story was in the *New York Times* ("Fight to Restore Rural Mail Route: 16 Vermont Families, with 4 Cars on Rationed Gas, Ask Washington for Justice"). We had enlisted the *New England Homestead*, the *Rural New Yorker* and other farm papers in the battle. We were just getting up steam on the third week of our campaign, when the Post Office Department announced the restoration of the valley's mail service.

Although this rather took the wind out of our sails, we at least could have a bang-up celebration. We got in touch with Mortimer Proctor, who was then Governor of Vermont, secured his consent to come to Jamaica, and arranged a victory party in the Jamaica Town Hall. "What? You've asked the Governor to come to Jamaica?" the townsfolk gasped. "Surely," the Committee answered, "Isn't he the Governor of Jamaica as well as other parts of Vermont?" The meeting was a great success. The hall was decorated; refreshments were served; the Governor and his wife attended, and a fine time was had by all. "It pays to holler," said one townsman; another shrewdly commented, "The wheel that squeaks the loudest gets the grease."

The theme of the celebration was the importance of building up rural areas. "The spirit that is in this room tonight," Governor Proctor said, "is the spirit of the Green Mountain Boys. You have the courage and perseverance and determination that the Green Mountain Boys had when they went down to the Continental Congress and presented the case for Vermont. When you presented your case in Washington, Washington recognized the kind of thunder that rolls out of Vermont when its spirit is aroused."

For the first and only time during our twenty years in the valley, the whole population, from "natives" to "outsiders," really worked together with a will. Cliques and animosities were forgotten. The episode provided a splendid example of the kind of community cooperation that was possible if people really made up their minds to do a job together.

"Now pause with yourselfe, and view the end of all your Labours . . . unspeakable Pleasure and infinite Commodity."

Gervase Markham, A New Orchard, 1648

"The ground is locked up, the farmer's exertions must relent, and now for him is the time to indulge in thinking and speculating upon what is passed and what is likely to come."

J. M. Gourgas, New England Farmer, January 25, 1828

"I went to the woods because I wished to live life deliberately, to front only the essential facts of life, and see if I could not learn what it had to teach, and not, when I came to die, discover that I had not lived. I did not wish to live what was not life, living is so dear; nor did I wish to practise resignation, unless it was quite necessary. I wanted to live deep and suck out all the marrow of life, to live so sturdily and spartan-like as to put to rout all that was not life, to cut a broad swath and shave close, to drive life into a corner, and reduce it to its lowest terms, and, if it proved to be mean, why then to get the whole and genuine meanness of it, and publish its meanness to the world; or if it were sublime, to know it by experience, and be able to give a true account of it in my next excursion."

Henry Thoreau, Walden, 1854

"He who digs a well, constructs a stone fountain, plants a grove of trees by the roadside, plants an orchard, builds a durable house, reclaims a swamp, or so much as puts a stone seat by the wayside, makes the land so far lovely and desirable, makes a fortune which he cannot carry away with him, but which is useful to his country long afterwards."

Ralph Waldo Emerson, Society and Solitude, 1870

"I do not think that any civilization can be called complete until it has progressed from sophistication to unsophistication, and made a conscious return to simplicity of thinking and living."

Lin Yutang, The Importance of Living, 1938

"When humanity gets tired enough of being hounded from pillar to post, when the powerful have sufficiently persecuted the weak and the envious weak have sufficiently obstructed the strong, perhaps our way of life will come to seem the true one, the good one; and people everywhere will awake in astonishment at having for so long neglected its simple wisdom."

Louise Dickinson Rich, My Neck of the Woods, 1950

CHAPTER 8

A BALANCE SHEET
OF THE VERMONT PROJECT

Social service, not escapism—Unified theory and practice
—Communal possibilities—Economic success—Visitors observe us—The valley's social inadequacy—Patternless living
the norm—Everyone for himself—Our individual stand

AGAIN and again people have asked us: "Why did you escape to
this idyllic spot? Why not stay in the noise, dirt and turmoil of
one of the great urban centers, sharing the misery and anguish of
your fellow humans?" We recognize the relevance of this question. Indeed, it extends to the social foundations upon which
those not satisfied with western civilization must strive to build
an alternative culture pattern. We would go further and agree
that this question reaches beyond sociology into the realm of
ethics. In several respects, it is the question of questions. Like
any basic social or ethical issue, it cannot be answered easily, nor
can it be met with a categorical reply. Any attempt at an inclusive
answer must contain exceptions and limitations.

Suppose we begin our answer to this perennial question by
admitting that in a remote Green Mountain valley one is not in

daily contact with the labor struggle, nor is he subject to the pressures of those who live, work, travel and recreate in New York, Chicago or San Francisco. The life in Vermont is different in texture from that of a metropolis. Is it "better" or "worse"? That depends upon the way in which the words are used. For us the life in Vermont was definitely better because it permitted frequent contacts with nature, because it afforded an opportunity to master and direct nature forces, because manual skills were still practiced and because the routine of living was less exacting. Instead of spending early and late hours in dirty, noisy, subway or train, we stayed on our own grounds week in and week out. Travelling to and from work, for us, meant walking two hundred yards from kitchen to saphouse. If snow was deep, the trip might require snowshoes or skis, but that was an advantage because it called for another skill.

This answer does not meet fully our central question: "Why should you avail yourself of these many advantages when fellow humans are deprived of them in city slums?" If we were compelled to answer this question categorically, we would say that under any and all conditions one is responsible for living as well as possible within the complex of circumstances which constitutes the day-to-day environment. Where there is a choice, with the evidence all recorded and the circumstances all considered, one chooses the better part rather than the worse.

Living is a business in which we all engage. In the course of the day, there are certain things we must do,—for example, breathe. There are also things we may do or may decide not to do,—such as, stay home and bake a cake, or go out and visit a friend. The center of life routine is surrounded by a circumference of choice. There is the vocation which provides livelihood, and the avocations which thrive on leisure and surplus energy.

A professional actor or musician must live close enough to his job to get there every working day. A poet or painter has a wider range from which to choose his living place. Under what obligation are these individuals to stay in the congested centers of population?

We would put the matter affirmatively. Since congestion is a social disadvantage, these individuals are in duty bound to avoid congested areas unless for some reason business or duty calls them there. If they go into the centers of population, instead of improving matters they make congestion worse.

We may state the issue in another way,—whatever the nature of one's beliefs, one's personal conduct may either follow the belief pattern or diverge from it. In so far as it diverges, it helps produce unwanted results. At the same time, it splits practice away from theory and divides the personality against itself. The most harmonious life is one in which theory and practice are unified.

From this it follows that each moment, hour, day, week and year should be treated as an occasion,—another opportunity to live as well as possible, in accordance with the old saying "Tomorrow is a new day" or the new Mexican greeting "Siempre mejor" (always better) in place of the conventional "Buenos dias" (good day). With body in health, emotions in balance, mind in tune and vision fixed on a better life and a better world, life, individually and collectively, is already better.

On this point we differ emphatically with many of our friends and acquaintances who say, in effect, "Never mind how we live today; we are in this dog-eat-dog social system and we may as well get what we can out of it. But tomorrow, in a wiser, more social and more humane world, we will live more rationally, more economically, more efficiently, more socially". Such talk is nonsense.

As we live in the present, so is our future shaped, channeled and largely determined.

Apply this thinking to our problem of living in the Green Mountains and believing in and working for a cooperative, peaceful, social order. Our life in Vermont may be justified, or can justify itself,—(1) as an instance and an example of sane living in an insane world; (2) as a means of contacting nature, a contact in many ways more important than contacting society; (3) as a desirable, limited alternative to one segment of the existing social order; (4) as a refuge for political deviants; (5) as a milieu in which heretofore active people can spend their riper years (in accordance with the Eastern conception of life stages: the sage or anchorite following the stage of householder); (6) as an opportunity for the sage or mature person to follow his profession and avocations.

Action has its advocates. Contemplation also has its adherents. The former tends to be exterior, peripheral or centrifugal; while the latter, by comparison, more inner, central and vital.

Perhaps we can summarize our point of view in this way. We are opposed to the theories of a competitive, acquisitive, aggressive, war-making social order, which butchers for food and murders for sport and for power. The closer we have to come to this social order the more completely are we a part of it. Since we reject it in theory, we should, as far as possible, reject it also in practice. On no other basis can theory and practice be unified. At the same time, and to the utmost extent, we should live as decently, kindly, justly, orderly and efficiently as possible. Human beings, under any set of circumstances, can behave well or badly. Whatever the circumstances, it is better to love, create and construct than to hate, undermine and destroy, or, what may be even worse at times, ignore and *laissez passer*. We believed that we could make our contribution to the good life more effectively in a pre-industrial, rural community than in one of the great urban centers.

During several decades we have been in close contact with like-minded men and women all through the United States who have tried the rural alternative and with others who have tried the urban alternative. We feel that both groups have made and are making a contribution. We still feel, however, as we did in 1932, that the rural alternative (the "small community" of Arthur E. Morgan, Baker Brownell and Ralph Borsodi) offers greater individual and collective constructive possibilities than the urban.

We are far from assuming that the ruralists will be able to set up a social communal alternative to capitalist urbanism. In the face of centuries of experience we did not assume that in 1932. We are surer now than we were then that these communities are confined rigidly to the few, rarely endowed and super-normally equipped men and women who are willing and able to live as altruists after being trained, conditioned and coerced by an acquisitive, competitive, ego-centric social system.[1]

What we did feel and what we still assert is that it is worthwhile for the individual who is rejected by a disintegrating urban community to formulate a theory of conduct and to put into practise a program of action which will enable him or her to live as decently as possible under existing circumstances.

Viewed in a long perspective, our Vermont project was a personal stop-gap, an emergency expedient. But in the short view it was a way of preserving self-respect and of demonstrating to the few who were willing to observe, listen and participate, that life in a dying acquisitive culture can be individually and socially

[1] For examples of attempts at organizing communal centers in the U.S., read V. F. Calverton's *Where Angels Dared To Tread*, N.Y.: Bobbs-Merrill 1941

purposeful, creative, constructive and deeply rewarding, provided that economic solvency and psychological balance are preserved.

Economically the successes achieved in the working out of the Vermont project far outweighed the failures. First and foremost, our idea of a subsistence homestead economy proved easy of realization. In exchange for a few months per year of carefully planned bread labor, we were able to provide ourselves with the bulk of our year's food. A few weeks of work furnished our house fuel. Another few weeks provided the needed repairs and replacements on buildings, tools and equipment. Capital replacement of housing (new stone buildings for old wooden ones) was a more extensive task, involving considerable outlays of planning, time, energy, persistence, materials and capital. Once a stone building was in place, however, the yearly cost of repairs and replacements fell almost to zero.

With this provision of necessaries went an unbelievable degree of good health, which is a matter of primary importance to people aiming at economic self-sufficiency on the one hand and social reconstruction on the other. Literally, we were always well, and on the rare occasions when the approaches of a cold appeared temporarily to lower our vitality, we followed the accepted practice of the cats and dogs of the neighborhood, and stopped eating until we felt fit. It is unnecessary for us to say that the difference between good health and bad is the difference between the success and failure of almost any long-term human project.

Life's necessaries are easily come by if people are willing to adjust their consumption to the quantity and variety of their products. Difficulties begin when the subsistence advocate enters the market with its lures and wiles for separating the unwary and the dullwitted from their medium of exchange. Never forget that from the private ownership of the means of production, through the monopoly of natural resources and patents, the control over money, the imposition of the tribute called "interest", the gambling centers which trade in commodities and "securities", to price control and the domination by the wealthlords of the agencies which shape men's minds and the machinery of government, the entire apparatus of a competitive, acquisitive, exploitive, coercive social order is rigged and manipulated for the rich and the powerful and against the poor and the weak. Keep out of the system's clutches and you have a chance of subsistence, even if the oligarchs disapprove of what you think and say and do. Accept the system, with its implications and ramifications, and you become a helpless cog in an impersonal, implacable, merciless machine operated to make rich men richer and powerful men more powerful.

As a means of providing a subsistence household with the cash necessary to buy out the market, to shop from one end of a mail order catalog to another or to provide the family with endless comforts, conveniences, labor-saving gadgets, trinkets and habit-forming drugs, our project was a dismal failure. It could not compete with the big show in the big tent of western culture. But if treated as a venture in economic self-containment and an experiment in economy, frugality, self-discipline and day-to-day training for a new way of life, our project was a real success. In that respect, we dare say that during the twenty years we spent on our Vermont enterprise we learned more things and more important things than we could have found out during twenty years in Harvard, Columbia and the University of California all rolled into one.

Among the many questions which were asked us while in Vermont, perhaps the most crucial one was: "If you were back in 1932, but knowing what you know today, would you do the whole thing over again?" Our answer to that question in an emphatic affirmative: "Most certainly we would!" We consider the time and energy put into the adventure as well spent. We do not know how we would go about spending them to better advantage under the circumstances prevailing in the United States from 1932 to 1952. For us, the two Vermont decades were an exciting, engrossing, enlightening, rewarding twenty years, which we were glad to share with our Vermont neighbors and the ceaseless stream of relatives, friends, acquaintances and utter strangers who knocked at our door.

Our early years in the valley brought few visitors. We were only newly established, and our address was not known. As folk began to find us out and travel up the dirt road to our door, they met a welcome, but accommodations were limited. The Ellonen house was not built for company. We put up all over-nighters in the nearby schoolhouse, furnished with only bare necessities.

When building our new house we included a guesthouse in the plans. With this and the rented schoolhouse we could, and did, accommodate a large shifting population of visitors all summer long. The existence of this surplus housing had magical drawing power. Lone wanderers, and families with dogs, cats and baggage arrived from nowhere and kept the rooms occupied. The doors were never locked. Anyone was welcome to occupy the guesthouse, and no one ever paid for room or board. It was, as some friends dubbed it, a "free inn". Many a morning, at breakfast, a whole family would stroll into our kitchen, "Good morning, we slept in your guesthouse last night." Then they would sit down for breakfast.

Ah, there came the rub. Most of them were in for a shock. No coffee, no cereal, no bacon, no eggs, no toast, no pancakes or maple syrup. Just apples, and sunflower seeds, and a black molasses drink. Such a fare sent many a traveller on his way soon enough.

M. G. Kains, in his well-deserved best-seller, *Five Acres and Independence,* describes his experiences with itinerate visitors. "After they have taken up farming, many a city man and his wife—particularly his wife!—have run the gamut of emotions through all the descending scale of delight, gratification, pleasure, surprise, perplexity, annoyance, disgust and exasperation (a full octave!) to discover how popular they have become since moving to the country. Not only do their intimate friends drop in un-announced on fine Sundays, but less and less intimate ones even down to people who just happened to live around the block, arrive in auto loads and all expect to remain for dinner, perhaps supper also! . . . As you will probably have to solve the same problem, let me tell you the answer: For Sunday dinners have corned beef and cabbage, beef stew or hash! Good luck to you!"[2] They came to us all days of the week and we served them raw cauliflower and boiled wheat! However, there were those of our way of living and eating who said they had with us some of the best meals of their lives.

There was another fact which tempered the felicity of our easy hospitality. "The busy Man has few idle Visitors; to the boiling Pot the Flies come not." We had certain things to do every day and we aimed to do them, come who would. We went about our jobs as usual and let guests fend for themselves, or come and help, if they wished. We served no iced tea on the terrace while telling or listening to life histories. By some we were thought uncordial, but we did not aim to entertain.

We learned to distinguish the drone from the worker. There were those who were hammock-liers (although we provided no

[2] N.Y.: Greenberg 1942 p. 9

hammocks), out for a vacation and a good time. They never stayed long. Our mattresses were not foam-rubber nor our coffee Maxwell House. Then there were those good souls, forever under foot, who were willing to help but incapable or too feeble. We liked them, but had to leave them, and unless they had inner resources they too left soon. A few—a very few, took hold and really fitted into our life pattern. They usually were in demand somewhere else and could not stay long enough. They were welcome again and again.

From all our guests we asked a minimum of consideration for ourselves and others, which included cooperation on household maintenance. We came to hope for very little in the way of assistance with bread labor, and perhaps it was too much to ask of worn-out, frazzled city-dwellers on vacation. We also came to realize that we should warn people before they arrived, entertaining false notions concerning our forest farmhouse. And so we evolved a form letter which we sent to inquirers who wrote and asked if they could come and stay a few days, a week or a month and more. It ran something like this:

"We are a small family working out a way of living, and at the same time earning a living. Our accommodations are built for that purpose only and we do not conduct an inn or a sanatarium or a vacation center. We work at bread labor at least four hours a day, plus the short time needed to get our simple, vegetarian meals. We all follow this daily routine and expect those who happen to stay here for a time to fit in. Meat, tobacco and alcohol are taboo on the place. Our living is simple and austere; some would say hard and comfortless. If you are ever passing this way, you are welcome to stop in. We are always glad to see people of our way of thinking and living, and to share with them whatever we have, do, feel and think."

More than nine-tenths of the hundreds of visitors who stopped at Forest Farms went away with the oral remark or the mental note: "Its a nice way to live if you can take it. Maybe such a life pattern is alright for them, but preserve me from having to endure it for any length of time". They admitted that we ate more wholesomely, and cheaper, than they did; our health was far better than most; we were adequately clothed and comfortably housed; we had time for leisure in beautiful surroundings; but as for themselves, they could not or would not discipline themselves; nor go without the excitement, the rush, the glamour, the gadgets and the soporifics of civilization. If they had stayed, they would have had to face the fact that subsistence living allows only a narrow margin of purchasing power for new cash capital outlays. This is one of the most drastic limitations in a society which insists upon changing and replacing tawdry, temporary capital goods with each invention or discovery or each new advertising campaign.

There was another matter of great importance, especially to young couples. Our set-up contained no small children and did not have to take into consideration their support or higher education. We believe that small children could have been accommodated in the economic and social apparatus of our project, without too much rearrangement and reorganization. But we are sure that as set up, it would not have permitted a parent to send a child to an expensive private school or finance his way through a professional course such as medicine. Such enterprises are possible for the well-to-do in urban centers. They are out of reach of the subsistence homesteader unless scholarships or outside work are possible for the would-be student.

If it were the place in this book, we would glady argue out the entire educational question, especially in its technical and professional phases, which, in the past few years, have been taken over so largely by the United States military authorities. Suffice it here to note that it is a high hurdle for those who wish to fit their offspring to succeed in the get-ahead-grab-and-keep competition of contemporary North America.

Considered in terms of individual health and happiness, our project was an emphatic success. Viewed socially, however, even on its economic side, it left much to be desired. Our household group, for instance, was relatively small,—never more than four or five adults, with a stream of visitors from the outside world who did not stay for long. When it came to planning, therefore, we suffered from the absence of varied viewpoints and varied experience. In the execution of plans the group lacked emulation and the stimulus that accompanies friendly rivalry. It suffered from the absence of diverse skills of many individuals. It also suffered from its small numbers when it came to doing big jobs of construction, wood cutting and the like. On such big jobs, teams of experienced people, accustomed to working together, can run circles around small groups of amateurs.

In the absence of effective neighborhood cooperation, the small size of the group deprived us of an opportunity for specialization and division of labor and placed an undue burden of varied chores and tasks upon each participant in the experiment. When two or more of the tasks demanded attention at the same time, the result might well have been strain, tension and dissipation of energy to no constructive purpose. Had our group consisted of a dozen or a score of capable adults, animated by the same purposes and willing to follow out agreed plans, along lines of well-established practice, our standard of living could have been attained and maintained with far less expenditure of energy and labor time, leaving much more time and energy for leisure and avocational interests.

The social inadequacy of our Vermont project is characteristic of all rural America, where separatism and individualism have subdivided the community almost to the point of sterility. We have said that there were too few of us to be economically effective, even in a simple economy based chiefly on hand tool agriculture and hand crafts. The social or sociological inadequacy of our group was even more pronounced.

Had we been able to integrate fifteen or twenty families of the immediate neighborhood into a well-knit unit, based economically on cooperation and mutual aid and socially on the principles of live and help live, not "mine for me" but "ours for us", the resulting community still would have been woefully deficient in a variety of complementary skills, talents and social relationships.

For example,—there would not have been enough good voices to make up a choir, not enough passable musicians to man a local orchestra or enough actors to set up an effective dramatic troupe or dance team. Or, viewed from another angle, there would not have been enough babies to warrant the organization of a nursery school or kindergarten, nor would there have been enough six-year olders for a first grade or enough teen-agers to establish and maintain a reasonable balanced social group at that difficult, unbalanced age.

Had the community undertaken to set up a dramatic club, a kindergarten or a teen-age group, it would have been compelled to augment its members by bringing in outsiders who were either indifferent or hostile to the ideological standards and social purposes of the community. Once the inflow of outsiders began, it would have been a matter of time before the life of the community would have been diluted or disrupted by unfriendly outside influences. This is exactly what did happen in the community center.

Skinner, in his *Walden Two*,[3] correctly stated the minimum social requirements for an intentional commune,—(1) enough people to provide variety, diversity and specialization; (2) sufficient control over ingress and egress to preserve ideological purity, group identity and group purpose. Our valley in southern Vermont, like virtually all rural America, was lacking in these minimum requirements for a balanced, autonomous community existence.

In one sense Vermont offered less rather than more opportunity for collective experiments than most other parts of rural America. Vermonters were strong individualists; the percentage of home ownership and farm ownership was unusually high; the population was thin and widely scattered, and all the major Vermont traditions emphasized the individualism of the Green Mountain folk. Inhabitants of our valley, like other rural Americans, were organized in autonomous households. "Autonomous" is hardly the word. "Sovereign" would be a more exact descriptive term.

Vermont life was "free" in the sense that it placed before the individual and the household a wide range of choices. There was no set pattern. The State of Vermont was scarcely in evidence. During the entire twenty years of our sojourn we never saw a uniformed policeman pass along the dirt road in front of our house. Once a year the town listers assessed property, but their visits were brief and perfunctory. From day to day and year to year we did as we pleased. Aside from our own thinking and direction, our lives need not have been planned or patterned.

There was a degree of neighborhood pressure toward social

[3] B. F. Skinner, N. Y.: Macmillan 1948

conformity. Otherwise we were our own masters so long as we paid our taxes and obeyed traffic laws on the state highways. The only management or discipline to which we were subject was self-imposed. In fact, the word "discipline" was in such disrepute among the families in the valley, that its mention aroused sharp opposition.

With minor exceptions every household group in the valley owned land, buildings and tools in fee simple. Each household was, to that extent, economically self-contained. Each was socially self-regulating. In a word, each household was a law unto itself and was based upon a solid economic foundation,—a piece of the earth from which, at a pinch, it could dig its own livelihood. Only the tax collector, the truant officer and the recruiting sergeant could break into the domestic castles. In extreme cases, the police, the sheriff and the game warden could invade the premises, but only on complaint or suspicion of flagrant law violation. In such cases, law enforcement personnel went in groups and armed, since practically every rural Vermonter kept firearms and a stock of ammunition.

There is no positive force, in rural Vermont or in rural America, drawing communities together for well-defined social purposes. Churches, parent-teacher associations, farm unions, granges, farm bureaus, cooperatives and improvement associations cover specified fields, and perform particular functions. No one of these groups deal with general rural welfare, even to the extent that the service clubs in trading towns and small cities deal with general urban welfare.

Someone may suggest that general welfare is the business of government, under the constitutions of Vermont and the United States. To a degree that is true, and the New England town meeting plays such a role in a restricted sense. Outside of New

England and a few border states, however, the town meeting has not existed, and in New England its functions have been sharply circumscribed by its infrequent, formal meetings and by the organization of rural life into sovereign households, each with its economic base in land ownership and each with its arsenal prepared to defend its individualism to the death.

Atomism, separatism and consequent isolation have increasingly played havoc with rural life in the United States as the family has decreased in size while the household has shed some of its most essential functions. Meanwhile rural mail routes, mail order houses, travelling markets and salesmen have joined hands with rural telephone lines, rural electrification, school consolidation, radio and television, mass auto production and good roads to link the rural communities to urban markets and urban shopping and recreation centers. The resulting absence of group spirit and neighborhood discipline, the chaos and confusion of perpetual movement to and from work, to and from school, to and from the shows and the dances, has destroyed the remnants of rural solidarity and left a shattered, purposeless, functionless, ineffective, unworkable community.

Against this all-pervasive decline and dissolution of the fragile, tenuous structure of America's rural community life we attempted to make a stand in the Pikes Falls valley, in Vermont. Our chances of success were about equal to those of an Alpinist who throws himself against an avalanche.

We are not writing this by way of self defense or self justification. Rather we are attempting to explain and to understand the determined, stubborn resistance of Green Mountain dwellers, in and near our valley, to every attempt at community integration and collective action. Socially our experiment was a failure because the social set-up doomed such an experiment before it was born.

Were we aware of these facts when me moved to Vermont in 1932? Certainly. We knew the social history of the United States; we had heard the issues discussed a hundred times. We did not know the detail as we encountered it in our efforts to build a local community in a disintegrating society. But had we known all and more, we would have persevered, because the value of doing something does not lie in the ease or difficulty, the probability or improbability of its achievement, but in the vision, the plan, the determination and the perseverance, the effort and the struggle which go into the project. Life is enriched by aspiration and effort, rather than by acquisition and accumulation. Knowing this, and despite the odds against success, if we had it to do over again we would attempt the Vermont project in its social as well as in its economic aspects.

"Thus gentle Reader I have (I trust) fully satisfied thy desire in as many things as are needful to be knowne: wherefore I commit my little Booke to thy gentle judgement. If thou maist receive any profit or commodities thereby, I shalbe glad to it: and if not, yet favorably let it pass from thee to others, whose knowledge and experience is lesse than thine therein, that they may gather such things as to them are strange, though to thee well knowne before."

Thomas Hill, The Arte of Gardening, 1608

AFTERWORD

NINETEEN YEARS of experimental homesteading in Vermont provided the material that went into the writing of *Living the Good Life*.

Eighteen years of homesteading in Maine have rounded out our Vermont experience, matured it, and assured us that the life possibilities which we had explored in the Green Mountains of Vermont were equally available on the coast of another New England state.

Countless people, young and old, have visited our Vermont and Maine homesteads. Many of them have been impressed by our way of life and have decided to try out homesteading on their own account. A sight of the place and us at work seems to add to what they have learned from the book, so we are happy to share our experience with them on the spot.

It is easy to add a bit of water to the soup to stretch it for a crowd or mix up some oats and oil and raisins for extra horse-chow when unexpected visitors drop in, but putting up people is another thing. In Maine we no longer have a guest house or space to lodge visitors, but we are glad to meet and talk with those who are earnestly seeking, who write to us in advance and come to Forest Farm at times convenient to them and to us. On any other basis numerous visitors would disrupt the daily routines of our good life.

HELEN and SCOTT NEARING

Harborside, Maine
April 1970

"The more I am acquainted with agricultural affairs, the better I am pleased with them; insomuch, that I can no where find so great satisfaction as in those innocent and useful pursuits. In indulging these feelings, I am led to reflect how much more delightful to an undebauched mind, is the task of making improvements on the earth, than all the vainglory which can be acquired from ravaging it, by the most uninterrupted career of conquests."

George Washington, Letter to Arthur Young December 4, 1788

"All gentlemen who make agriculture their business or amusement, should register their trials and either publish them themselves, or communicate them to others who will take that trouble. It is inconceivable how much the world would be benefited by such a conduct; matters relative to rural economics would receive a new face; every day would bring forth some valuable discovery, and every year that passed yield such an increase of knowledge, as to point and smooth the way to discoveries now unthought of. . . . As far as a man's fortune will allow him to go, no amusement in the world equals the forming and conducting experiments in agriculture; to those, I mean, who have a taste for rural matters; nor can any business, however, important, exceed, in real utility, this amusement. Experiments that are made with spirit and accuracy, are of incomparable value in every branch of natural philosophy; those of agriculture, which is the most useful of those branches, must be particularly valuable."

Arthur Young, Rural Economy, 1792

"Before a man attempts the history of any subject, he ought to know it well; and those who undertake to write upon the economy of a country, would do well to wait till they had been long enough in one place to forget the many prejudices they had brought with them; and if their object be truly to instruct, they should endeavour to do it by example, which is the strongest lesson; and they will be readily followed if they can once shew to those in whose interest they take concern, that they have known how to manage their own."

Judge William Cooper, A Guide in the Wilderness, 1810

"The discoveries in the cultivation of the earth are not confined to the time and country in which they are made, but may be considered as extending to future ages, and intended to meliorate the condition of the whole human race, and providing subsistence and enjoyment for generations yet unborn."

Leonard E. Lathrop, The Farmer's Library, 1826

BIBLIOGRAPHY

Aldrich, Chilson D., *The Real Log Cabin*, N.Y.: Macmillan, 1928.

Baker, O. E.; Borsodi, Ralph and Wilson, M. L., *Agriculture in Modern Life*, N.Y.: Harper, 1939

Balfour, Eve Balfour, *The Living Soil*, London: Faber & Faber, 1949

Barborka, Clifford J., *Treatment by Diet*, Philadelphia: Lippincott, 1936

Barr, Stringfellow, *The Pilgrimage of Western Man*, N.Y.: Harcourt Brace, 1949

Booth, Edward Townsend, *Country Life in America*, N.Y.: Knopf, 1947

———, *God Made the Country*, N.Y.: Knopf, 1946

Borsodi, Ralph, *Flight from the City*, N.Y.: Harper, 1933

———, *This Ugly Civilization*, N.Y.: Simon & Schuster, 1929

Brimmer, F. E., *Camps, Log Cabins, Lodges and Clubhouses*, N.Y.: Appleton, 1925

Bromfield, Louis, *Pleasant Valley*, N.Y.: Harper, 1945

Brownell, Baker, *The Human Community*, N.Y.: Harper, 1950

———, and Wright, F. L., *Architecture and Modern Life*, N.Y.: Harper, 1938

Carque, Otto, *Natural Foods*, Los Angeles, California: Carque, 1926

———, *Rational Diet*, Los Angeles, California: Times Mirror Press, 1926

Cary, Harold, *Build a Home—Save a Third*, N.Y.: Reynolds, 1924

Colby, Evelyn and Forrest, John G., *Ways and Means to Successful Retirement* N.Y.: Forbes & Sons, 1952

Corey, Paul, *Build a Home*, N.Y.: Dial, 1946

———, *Buy an Acre*, N.Y.: Dial, 1944

Cruikshank, E. W. H., *Food and Nutrition*, Toronto: Macmillan, 1946

Davis, Adelle, *Let's Cook It Right*, N.Y.: Harcourt, Brace, 1947

———, *Vitality through Planned Nutrition*, N.Y.: Macmillan, 1949

Demarquette, Jacques, *Le Naturisme Integral*, Paris: Editions du Trait d'Union 1931

Dempsey, Paul W., *Grow Your Own Vegetables*, Boston: Houghton Mifflin, 1942

Evelyn, John, *A Philosophic Discourse on Earth*, London: Martyn, 1676

Faulkner, Edward H., *Plowman's Folly*, Norman: University of Oklahoma, 1943

Fed, Rockwell F., *10,000 Garden Questions*, N.Y.: Doubleday Doran, 1944

Flagg, Ernest, *Small Houses: Their Economic Design and Construction*, N.Y.: Scribners, 1922

Gannet, Lewis, *Cream Hill*, N.Y.: Viking, 1949

Gould, John, *The House that Jacob Built*, N.Y.: Morrow, 1947

Greenberg, David B. and Corbin, Charles, *So You're Going to Buy a Farm*, N.Y.: Greenberg, 1944

Gregg, Richard, *Voluntary Simplicity*, Wallingford, Pa.: Pendle Hill, 1930

Greiner, T., *How to Make the Garden Pay*, Philadelphia, Maule, 1890

Gustafson, Hardenburg, *Land for the Family, A Guide to Country Living*, Ithaca, N.Y.: Comstock, 1947

Hambidge, Gove, *Enchanted Acre*, N.Y.: McGraw Hill, 1925

——, *Time to Live*, N.Y.: McGraw Hill, 1933

Hay, William Howard, *Health via Food*, N.Y.: Sun-Diet Press, 1930

——, *Some Human Ailments*, Mt. Pocono, Pa.: Pocono Haven, 1937

——, *Superior Health through Nutrition*, N.Y.: Hay, 1944

Highstone, H. A., *Practical Farming for Beginners*, N.Y.: Harper, 1940

Godgins, Eric, *Mr. Blandings Builds his Dream House*, N.Y.: Simon & Schuster, 1946

Hopkins, Donald P., *Chemicals, Humus and the Soil*, N.Y.: Chemical Pub. Co., 1948

Howard, Albert, *An Agricultural Testament*, London: Oxford University Press, 1940

——, *The Soil and Health*, N.Y.: Devin-Adair, 1952

Hyams, Edward, *Soil and Civilization*, London: Thames & Hudson, 1952

James, George Wharton, *The Indians' Secrets of Health*, Pasadena, California: Radiant Life, 1917

Jensen, Anton H., *How to Eat Safely in a Poisoned World*, Lincoln, Neb.: Jensen, 1949

Jones, H. A. and Emsweller, S. L., *The Vegetable Industry*, N.Y.: McGraw Hill, 1931

Kaighn, Raymond P., *How to Retire and Like It*, N.Y.: Association Press, 1951

Kains, Maurice Grenville, *Five Acres and Independence*, N.Y.: Greenberg, 1935

Kallet, Arthur and Schlink, F. J., *100,000,000 Guinea Pigs*, N.Y.: Vanguard, 1933

Kellogg, Charles E., *The Soils that Support Us*, N.Y.: Macmillan, 1941

Kemp, Oliver, *Wilderness Homes*, N.Y.: Outing Pub. Co., 1908

King, F. H., *Farmers of Forty Centuries*, N.Y.: Harcourt Brace, 1927

Kingsford, Anna, *The Perfect Way in Diet*, London: Kegan Paul, 1904

Lindlahr, Henry, *The Practice of Nature Cure*, N. Y.: Nature Cure Library, 1931

Lindlahr, Victor H., *The Natural Way to Health*, N.Y.: Natural Nutrition Society, 1939

———, *You Are What You Eat*, N.Y.: Natural Nutrition Society, 1942

Lovell, Philip M., *Diet for Health by Natural Methods*, Los Angeles: Times Mirror, 1931

———, *The Health of the Child by Natural Methods*, Los Angeles: Times Mirror, 1927

McCann, Alfred W., *This Famishing World*, N.Y.: Doubleday Doran, 1918

———, *The Science of Eating*, N.Y.: Doubleday Doran, 1931

McCarrison, R., *Nutrition and National Health*, London: Faber & Faber, 1944

———, *Studies in Deficiency Diseases*, Milwaukee, Wis.: Lee Foundation for Nutritional Research, 1945

Monier-Williams, George, *Trace Elements in Food*, N.Y.: Wiley, 1949

Morgan, Arthur E., *A Business of My Own*, Yellow Springs, Ohio: Community Service, 1946

Mumford, Lewis, *The Condition of Man*, N.Y.: Harcourt Brace, 1944

Nearing, Scott, *Economics for the Power Age*, N.Y.: John Day, 1952

———, *Where is Civilization Going?*, N.Y.: Vanguard, 1926

———, and Helen Nearing, *The Maple Sugar Book*, N.Y.: John Day, 1950

Norman, N. Philip, *Constructive Meal Planning*, Passaic, N.J.: Phototone Press, 1946

Ogden, Samuel R., *How to Grow Food for Your Family*, N.Y.: Barnes, 1943

———, *This Country Life*, N.Y.: Barnes, 1946

Osborn, Fairfield, *Our Plundered Planet*, Boston: Little, Brown, 1948

Paine, Lansing M. and Webster, Polly, *Start Your Own Business on Less than $1000*, N.Y.: McGraw Hill, 1950

Payne, Roger, *Why Work?*, Boston: Meador, 1939

Peters, Frazier Norman, *Pour Yourself a House*, N.Y.: McGraw Hill, 1949

———, *Without Benefit of Architect*, N.Y.: Putnam, 1937

Peterson, Elmer T., *Cities are Abnormal*, Norman, Okl.: University of Oklahoma Press, 1946

———, *Forward to the Land*, Norman, Okl.: University of Oklahoma Press, 1942

Pfeiffer, Ehrenfried, *Bio-Dynamic Farming and Gardening*, N.Y.: Anthroposophic Press, 1938

———, *Soil Fertility*, London: Faber & Faber, 1949

———, *The Earth's Face and Human Destiny*, Emmaus, Pa.: Rodale, 1947

Picton, Lionel James, *Nutrition and the Soil*, N.Y.: Devin Adair, 1949

Preston, John Frederick, *Developing Farm Woodlands*, N.Y.: McGraw Hill, 1954

Price, W. A., *Nutrition and Physical Degeneration*, N.Y.: Hoeber, 1939

Quigley, D. T., *The National Malnutrition*, Milwaukee, Wis.: Lee Foundation for Nutritional Research, 1948

Richter, John T., *Nature—the Healer*, West Haven, Conn.: Nature's Products, 1949

Roberts, Isaac Phillips, *10 Acres Enough*, N.Y.: Miller, 1864

Rochester, Anna, *Why Farmers are Poor*, N.Y.: International, 1940

Rodale, J. I., *The Organic Front*, Emmaus, Pa.: Rodale, 1949

———, *Pay Dirt*, N.Y.: Devin Adair, 1945

Rorty, James and Norman, N. P., *Tomorrow's Food*, N.Y.: Prentice Hall, 1947

Sanderson, L. D., *Rural Community*, N.Y.: Ginn, 1932

Scott, Cyril, *Health, Diet and Commonsense*, London: Homeopathic Pub. Co., 1950

Shelton, Herbert M., *The Hygienic System*, San Antonio, Texas: Shelton, 1947

Shepard, Ward, *Food or Famine*, N.Y.: Macmillan, 1945

Sigerist, Henry E., *Civilization and Disease*, N.Y.: Cornell University Press, 1945

Skinner, B. F., *Walden Two*, N.Y.: Macmillan, 1948

Sorokin, Pitrim A., *The Crisis of Our Age*, N.Y.: Dutton, 1949

———, *Man and Society in Calamity*, N.Y.: Dutton, 1942

Stannard, Stella, *Whole Grain Cookery*, N.Y.: John Day, 1951

Sternberg, Fritz, *The Coming Crisis*, N.Y.: John Day, 1947

Stevens, Henry Bailey, *The Recovery of Culture*, N.Y.: Harper, 1949

Stowell, Robert F., *Toward Simple Living*, Hartland, Vt.: Solitarian Press, 1953

Sutherland, G. A., *A System of Diet and Dietetics*, N.Y.: Physicians and Surgeons Book Co., 1925

Sykes, Friend, *Food, Farming and the Future*, Emmaus, Pa.: Rodale, 1951

———, *Humus and the Farmer*, London: Faber & Faber, 1946

Szekely, Edmond B., *Cosmotherapy, the Medicine of the Future*, Los Angeles: International Cosmotherapeutic Expedition, 1938

Thompson, Homer C., *Vegetable Crops*, N.Y.: McGraw Hill, 1939

Tilden, J. H., *Food*, Denver, Colorado: Tilden, 1914

Toynbee, Arnold, *Civilization on Trial*, N.Y.: Oxford, 1948

Tyler, Fred, *Plan for Independence*, N.Y.: Harian, 1951

Van de Water, F. F., *A Home in the Country*, N.Y.: Reynal, 1937
———, *We're Still in the Country*, N.Y.: John Day, 1938
Vogt, William, *Road to Survival*, N.Y.: Sloane, 1948
Wagner, Charles, *The Simple Life*, N.Y.: McClure, Phillips, 1904
Waksman, Selman H., *Soil Microbiology*, N.Y.: Wiley, 1952
Walker, Roy, *The Golden Feast*, N.Y.: Macmillan, 1952
Wend, Milton, *How to Live in the Country without Farming*, N.Y.: Doubleday Doran, 1944
Wrench, G. T., *The Wheel of Health*, London: Daniel, 1941
Wicks, William S., *Log Cabins*, N.Y.: Forest & Stream Pub. Co., 1889
Williams, Howard, *The Ethics of Diet*, London: James, 1907
Wilson, Charles Morrow, *Country Living*, Brattleboro, Vt.: Stephen Daye, 1938
Wright, Frank Lloyd, *On Architecture*, N.Y.: Duel, Sloane & Pearce, 1941
———, and Brownell, Baker, *Architecture and Modern Life*, Harper, 1938
Young, Arthur, *Rural Economy*, Burlington, Vt.: Neale, 1792
Young, Mildred Binns, *Functional Poverty*, Wallingford, Pa.: Pendle Hill, 1935
———, *Participation in Rural Life*, Wallingford, Pa.: Pendle Hill, 1940

ADDENDUM

Alcott, William A., *Ways of Living on Small Means*, Boston: Light & Stearns, 1837
———, *The Young House-Keeper, or, Thoughts on Food and Cookery*, Boston: George W. Light, 1842
———, *The Young Woman's Guide to Excellence*, N.Y.: Clark, Austin & Smith, 1852

Anon., *How a Small Income May Be Made to Go Far in a Family,* London: Fry, 1745

————, *Six Hundred Dollars a Year: A Wife's Effort at Low Living Under High Prices,* Boston: Tichnor & Fields, 1867

————, *The Young Housewife's Book, or, How to Eke Out a Small Income and Insure Domestic Happiness and Plenty on a Limited Scale of Expenditure,* N.Y.: Garrett, 1851

Beecher, Catherine E., *A Treatise on Domestic Economy,* Boston: Marsh, Capen, 1841

Copley, Esther, *Cottage Comforts, with Hints for Promoting Them, Gleaned from Experience,* London: Simpkin & Marshall, 1832

Cruger, Mary, *How She Did It, or, Comfort on $150 a Year,* N.Y.: Appleton, 1888

Culverwell, Dr. Robert James, *How to Be Happy (An Admonitory Essay),* N.Y.: Redfield, 1850

Lyman, Laura & Joseph, *How to Live: The Philosophy of Housekeeping,* Philadelphia: Thompson, 1882

Owen, Catherine, *Ten Dollars Enough (Keeping House Well on Ten Dollars a Week; How It Has Been Done; How It May be Done Again),* Boston: Houghton Mifflin, 1887

Robinson, Solon, *How to Live, or, Domestic Economy Illustrated,* N.Y.: Fowler & Wells, 1860

Warren, Eliza, *Comfort for Small Incomes,* Boston: Loring, 1866

————, *How I Managed My House on $1000 a Year,* Boston: Loring, 1866

INDEX